HUNTER H

EXPLORERS OF THE LATE RENAISSANCE AND THE ENLIGHTENMENT

FROM SIR FRANCIS DRAKE
TO MUNGO PARK

THE BRITANNICA GUIDE TO EXPLORERS AND ADVENTURERS

EXPLORERS OF THE LATE RENAISSANCE AND THE ENLIGHTENMENT

FROM SIR FRANCIS DRAKE TO MUNGO PARK

EDITED BY KENNETH PLETCHER, SENIOR EDITOR, GEOGRAPHY

Britannica Educational Publishing

IN ASSOCIATION WITH

ROSEN EDUCATIONAL SERVICES

Published in 2014 by Britannica Educational Publishing
(a trademark of Encyclopædia Britannica, Inc.) in association with Rosen Educational Services, LLC
29 East 21st Street, New York, NY 10010.

Copyright © 2014 Encyclopædia Britannica, Inc. Britannica, Encyclopædia Britannica, and the Thistle logo are registered trademarks of Encyclopædia Britannica, Inc. All rights reserved.

Rosen Educational Services materials copyright © 2014 Rosen Educational Services, LLC. All rights reserved.

Distributed exclusively by Rosen Educational Services.
For a listing of additional Britannica Educational Publishing titles, call toll free (800) 237-9932.

First Edition

Britannica Educational Publishing
J.E. Luebering: Director, Core Reference Group
Adam Augustyn: Assistant Manager, Core Reference Group
Marilyn L. Barton: Senior Coordinator, Production Control
Steven Bosco: Director, Editorial Technologies
Lisa S. Braucher: Senior Producer and Data Editor
Yvette Charboneau: Senior Copy Editor
Kathy Nakamura: Manager, Media Acquisition
Kenneth Pletcher, Senior Editor, Geography

Rosen Educational Services
Shalini Saxena: Editor
Nelson Sá: Art Director
Cindy Reiman: Photography Manager
Brian Garvey: Designer, Cover Design
Introduction by Richard Barrington

Library of Congress Cataloging-in-Publication Data

Explorers of the Late Renaissance and the Enlightenment: from Sir Francis Drake to Mungo Park/edited by: Ken Pletcher.—First Edition.
　　pages cm.—(The Britannica Guide to Explorers and Adventurers)
"In association with Britannica Educational Publishing, Rosen Educational Services."
Includes bibliographical references and index.
ISBN 978-1-62275-020-7 (library binding)
 1. Explorers—Biography. 2. Discoveries in geography. I. Pletcher, Kenneth, editor.
G200.E885 2013
910.92'2—dc23

2012043124

Manufactured in the United States of America

On the cover: An antique brass telescope and compass lying on a sea coast. *Sergej Razvodovskij/Shutterstock.com*

Cover, p. iii (ornamental graphic) © iStockphoto.com/Angelgild; interior pages (scroll) © iStockphoto.com/U.P. Images, (background texture) © iStockphoto.com/Peter Zelei

Contents

Introduction	viii
Pedro Menéndez de Avilés	1
Richard Chancellor	3
John Dee	4
Sir John Hawkins	7
Sir Martin Frobisher	9
Sir Humphrey Gilbert	10
Sir Francis Drake	12
Willem Barents	22
John Davis	23
Sir Walter Raleigh	24
Thomas Cavendish	29
Sir Richard Hawkins	30
William Adams	31
Pedro Páez	34
Henry Hudson	34
Samuel de Champlain	40
Sir Thomas Button	45
Dirck Hartog	46
John Smith	47
William Baffin	52
Anthony van Diemen	53
Jean Nicolet	54
Abel Janszoon Tasman	55
Semyon Ivanov Dezhnyov	59
Louis Hennepin	59
Jacques Marquette	60
Daniel Greysolon, sieur DuLhut	62
Pierre-Esprit Radisson	64
René-Robert Cavelier, sieur de La Salle	65
William Penn	71

13

36

56

Louis Jolliet	81
Henri de Tonty	82
William Dampier	83
Henry Kelsey	85
Vitus Bering	86
Pierre Gaultier de Varennes et de La Vérendrye	88
Charles-Marie de La Condamine	89
John Byron	91
James Cook	92
Louis-Antoine de Bougainville	99
James Bruce	102
Carsten Niebuhr	103
Daniel Boone	104
Arthur Phillip	107
Jean-François de Galaup, comte de La Pérouse	108
Sir Joseph Banks, Baronet	110
Samuel Hearne	112
Georg Forster	114
George Vancouver	115
Sir Alexander Mackenzie	117
George Bass	118
Mungo Park	119
Matthew Flinders	122
Conclusion	123
Glossary	126
Bibliography	129
Index	132

INTRODUCTION

In the early Renaissance, explorers sailed off the maps of the day, beyond the limits of what was known to their civilization. As a result, by the mid-1500s, most of the world's large, habitable land masses had been discovered, and Earth itself had been circumnavigated. Thus, educated people of the time had a reasonable outline of what their planet looked like. It was up to explorers of the late Renaissance and Enlightenment to fill in most of that outline.

Explorers of the late Renaissance and the subsequent period known as the Enlightenment did not so much discover new wholly unknown lands as explore the potential of places that were still a mystery to people of the time. By searching and surveying, they learned which areas had fertile lands, navigable rivers, and valuable natural resources. As a result of these efforts, explorers of the late Renaissance and the Enlightenment helped determine where hundreds of millions of people live today.

History owes a great debt to these intrepid souls, but their motives and methods were not always noble. They were often in search of wealth for themselves and conquest for the countries they served, and as a result some had little regard for the rights and lives of the native peoples they

Introduction

found in the lands they explored. This makes it a complicated period of history. For example, Pedro Menéndez de Avilés has a lasting place in history as founder of the oldest city in the United States: St. Augustine in what is now Florida. Nonetheless, he was also a brutal military commander who in at least one instance slaughtered his vanquished enemies. This was just one example of the steep price some would pay for European supremacy in North America.

Map of the world entitled "Nova Totius Terrarum Orbis Geographica ac Hydrographica Tabula," created by Dutch cartographer Henricus Hondius, 1630. DEA Picture Library /De Agostini/Getty Images

Explorers of the Late Renaissance and the Enlightenment: From Sir Francis Drake to Mungo Park

While some explorers of the late Renaissance were establishing the footholds for what were to become Europe's colonial empires, others were intent on furthering trade around the world. These ventures also have a mixed history—while many resulted in trade agreements that helped foster new relationships among nations, they also introduced the slave trade between Africa and the Americas and gave rise to a predatory class of sea explorers known as privateers. Privateers were essentially pirates sanctioned by a country and given license to prey on the ships of enemy countries in exchange for whatever wealth they found on board.

Whether a privateer was considered a hero or a rogue depended on each country's point of view, and some privateers achieved legendary status. Such was the case with Sir Francis Drake of England, a privateer in the latter part of the 16th century, when Queen Elizabeth I ruled England. Like many of his contemporaries, Drake made his fortune by plundering the ships and possessions of other countries, though he did it in a more spectacular fashion than most. After becoming the first Englishman to sail between the Atlantic and Pacific oceans via the Strait of Magellan at the southern tip of South America, Drake would ultimately become the second sea captain to circumnavigate the globe. First, though, he took advantage of the element of surprise to enrich himself and to strike a blow to Spain, then England's greatest adversary.

Prior to Drake's voyage, only Spanish ships had made it to the western side of South America. Although his expedition was down to one small ship at that point, Drake succeeded in raiding unsuspecting Spanish settlements and ships sailing along the Pacific coast of South America. Drake's exploits were among several factors that elevated tensions between England and Spain, and by the late 1580s the Spanish were preparing to invade England

Introduction

with a massive fleet—the Spanish Armada. (Drake's name would become forever linked with England's defeat of the Armada, though his role in the victory seems to have been limited to leading a raid that damaged the fleet in advance of the attempted invasion.) Drake's career is a prominent example of how some explorers of the era walked a thin line between ruthless pirate and national hero.

Drake's feat of sailing west and south to reach the Pacific Ocean was still unusual for its time because the journey was long and dangerous. Some explorers in the late 16th century began to seek an alternate route, known as the Northwest Passage. The idea was to sail north of the North American landmass and find a faster route to the Pacific via the Arctic Ocean. This objective was of particular interest to explorers from northern European nations such as the Netherlands and England, as these nations would have the most direct access to a northern sea route.

Ultimately, the Northwest Passage proved to be elusive, despite the efforts of explorers such as Willem Barents and Henry Hudson. Still, efforts to find that route cannot be dismissed as complete failures because they led to advances in navigation and to more precise charting of the northern seaways. These advances in the science of exploration were consistent with the Enlightenment, a period of intellectual discovery that followed the Renaissance in Europe in the 17th and 18th centuries.

Other changes were taking place as the late Renaissance era gave way to the Enlightenment. Whether it was the exploits of privateers or the discoveries of determined navigators, much of the exploration of the 1500s took place by sea. As the next century began, European powers began to eye settling and colonizing their recent discoveries, so exploration increasingly took place on land. Because their ships and sailors had led the way to North and South America, the British, Dutch, Spanish, Portuguese, and

French all had claims in the New World. At this point, the story of exploration became in part a race for territory.

One of the noteworthy early colonizers was John Smith, whose administrative skills were instrumental to the survival of England's Jamestown settlement at the beginning of the 17th century in what is now Virginia. While his encounter with Pocahontas may be more legend than fact, one of the ways Smith distinguished himself was by trying to cultivate constructive relationships with Native American tribes, rather than simply defeating them through force.

While there was much colonial interest in the New World, some European adventurers turned their attention to the south and to the east instead. Missionary work emerged as a new motivation for exploration alongside trade and territorial conquest in places such as Africa. Meanwhile, to the east, Australia and New Zealand were being more thoroughly explored, and the Dutch used conquest more than exploration to expand their extensive holdings in East and Southeast Asia, including parts of the East Indies (Indonesia), Ceylon (Sri Lanka), and Taiwan. Trade was the prominent reason for Dutch interest in Asia. Prominent explorers such as Anthony Van Diemen and Abel Tasman conducted their expeditions on behalf of the Dutch East India Company, which was granted a trading monopoly in the region by the Dutch government and often functioned as a de facto national navy there.

In the late 17th century, at around the time the Dutch were expanding their power base in Asia, the French were establishing a firm presence in North America. Frenchmen like Jacques Marquette and Pierre-Esprit Radisson expanded exploration inland, to the Great Lakes region and upper Mississippi River Valley. A little later, René-Robert Cavalier, sieur de La Salle, continued these voyages down the Mississippi, making the initial French claim on what would become the Louisiana Territory.

Introduction

The French expansion of their North American territory was primarily driven by trading interests, though there was also a strong missionary effort to bring Christianity to the various Native American tribes they encountered. Like England's John Smith in Jamestown, much of the French approach to Native Americans involved not driving them out of the territories but forging an understanding with them. The French took this further than Smith, however, as they formed alliances with some Indian tribes to enlist their help in fighting their Spanish and English colonial rivals as well as hostile Indian tribes.

Missionary work was not the only religious reason that explorers and adventurers came to the New World. A group of dissenting Protestants known as the Pilgrims came to what is now Massachusetts in the 1620s, followed in the 1630s by the Puritans. In the late 1600s, William Penn, an English Quaker, came to America in search of religious freedom after having spent time imprisoned in the Tower of London for publicizing his controversial beliefs. Penn founded Pennsylvania and became its first governor. His constitution for Pennsylvania included provisions for religious freedom and the passage of future amendments, which meant that Penn introduced elements that would become significant foundations of the United States Constitution a century later.

Not all exploration of North America emanated from the East Coast. In the early 1700s, Vitus Bering, a Dane sailing under the flag of Russia, explored the strait between Siberia and Alaska that now bears his name. Bering's survey of the Alaskan coastline led to Russia establishing a foothold in North America that would last until Alaska was purchased by the United States in 1867.

While explorers pressed more and more into the interiors of the North and South American continents, there remained a vast expanse of sea yet to be explored in the world's largest ocean, the Pacific. The most prominent individual to tackle this challenge in the late 1700s was Captain James Cook.

Sailing for the British Navy, Cook discovered several islands and made the first detailed charts of areas that were only vaguely known at the time. Most of this activity took place in the South Pacific, but Cook did sail south of the Antarctic Circle, though he never spotted the icy continent itself. Cook's expeditions are significant for other reasons. Up to that point, exploration had yielded primarily geographic or navigational information, but in Cook's case there were broader scientific benefits. In 1768 Cook commanded the *Endeavour* on the first scientific expedition to the Pacific, a mission that included botanists and astronomers. On a practical scientific note, Cook is recognized as the first naval commander to systematically avoid an outbreak of scurvy among his crew, which he accomplished by insisting on a specially designed diet that included limes and other citrus fruit.

Cook's was not the only expedition to feature a scientific element. In the late 1700s scientists regularly joined explorers on expeditions, whether to the Pacific by sea or the interior of Africa by land. In keeping with the spirit of the Enlightenment, exploration was no longer just a search for land and treasure, but it was increasingly a search for knowledge.

By the late 1700s, the great seas and land masses of the world had been discovered, but all too often few details had been recorded. That began to change, as the focus of many expeditions in the late 1700s was less on finding new lands than on surveying the features of areas that previously had been visited only briefly. Thus, details on coastlines, rivers, and other geographic features began to emerge. This type of knowledge helped clear the way for increased travel to these areas, and eventually to settlement in many cases.

Introduction

Besides wealth and knowledge, there was one other thing that explorers of this period regularly brought back with them: tales of their adventures. Books about exploration were very popular, making men like Captain Cook into legends, and helping to fuel further interest in exploration.

One of the more unusual motivations for voyaging to new lands involved Australia, where the purpose of the first permanent European settlement was to house convicts deported from Britain. Exploration and the expansion of knowledge were making the world a smaller place, but when the first prison colony was established there in 1788, the world still seemed vast enough that a nation felt it could get rid of some of its problems by sending them halfway across the globe. Other countries followed this example by establishing prison colonies in remote locations.

As noted previously, the period covered by this book was one in which explorers filled in much of the outline of what was known about the world. They did this in a literal sense by adding details to maps and charts, so far-off lands and seas went from being vague blotches or blank spaces to clearly defined shapes with recognizable features. They also filled in that outline with knowledge about science and about the wide variety of peoples and customs around the world.

From privateers to missionaries, from fur traders to scientists, explorers of the late Renaissance and the Enlightenment came in many different forms. By modern standards, there is much to find shocking in the way some of them acted and behaved. They could be ruthless, greedy, and vain, but it is also true that without their daring, knowledge about the world would be sadly lacking, and many of today's great cities and countries might not exist.

Pedro Menéndez de Avilés

(b. February 15, 1519, Avilés, Spain—
d. September 17, 1574, Santander)

The Spanish nobleman, seaman, and adventurer Pedro Menéndez de Avilés founded St. Augustine, Florida, the oldest continually settled city in what is now the United States. He was a classic example of the conquistador—intrepid, energetic, loyal, and brutal.

Born into the landed gentry, he ran away to sea at age 14. In 1549 he was commissioned by the Holy Roman emperor Charles V (Charles I of Spain) to drive pirates from the coasts of Spain. Five years later he was appointed captain of the West Indies fleet. An impatient man who acted with dispatch and reluctantly concerned himself with administrative details, he made numerous enemies, who brought about his imprisonment in 1563. He was freed two years later after he had regained royal favour.

Because King Philip II (Charles's son and successor) was disturbed by the potential threat to Spain's possessions from a settlement of French Huguenots (Protestants) on a strategic part of Florida's Atlantic coast, he sent Menéndez de Avilés to Florida to establish a colony there and deal with the French. The expedition sailed in July 1565 with 11 ships and about 2,000 men. On August 28 he entered and named the bay of St. Augustine and built a fort there. On September 20 he took the nearby French colony of Fort Caroline and massacred the entire population, hanging the bodies on trees with the inscription

Statue of Pedro Menéndez de Avilés outside of the Alcazar Hotel in St. Augustine, Fla. Dennis K. Johnson/Lonely Planet Images/Getty Images

"Not as Frenchmen, but as heretics." Menéndez de Avilés then explored the Atlantic coast and established a string of forts as far north as the island of St. Helena (off present-day South Carolina). He was recalled to Spain in 1567 and later helped organize a squadron of ships against the English. He died while engaged in this task.

Richard Chancellor

(d. November 10, 1556, Pitsligo Bay, Aberdeen, Scotland)

Richard Chancellor was a mid-16th-century British seaman. He is remembered for his visit to Moscow in 1553–54, which laid the foundations for English trade with Russia.

In 1553 Chancellor was appointed pilot general of Sir Hugh Willoughby's expedition in search of a Northeast Passage from England to China. The three-vessel fleet was to rendezvous at Vardø, Norway, but because of stormy weather Chancellor's was the only ship to make it to Vardø. Willoughby and his crew died in Lapland (northern Scandinavia), but Chancellor continued on into the White Sea, then journeyed overland to Moscow. There Tsar Ivan IV greeted him with warm hospitality and gave him a letter granting the English favourable conditions for trade with Russia. Chancellor rejoined his ship in the summer of 1554 and returned to England. His successful negotiations with the tsar resulted in the formation (1555) of the Muscovy Company, which was given a monopoly of Russian trade.

From October 1555 to July 1556 Chancellor was again in Moscow on a trading mission, but on the return voyage he lost his life in a shipwreck off the northeast coast of Scotland.

John Dee

(b. July 13, 1527, London, England—
d. December 1608, Mortlake, Surrey,
or March 26, 1609, London)

John Dee was an English mathematician, natural philosopher, and student of the occult. For many years he was an adviser to those undertaking long ocean voyages.

Dee entered St. John's College, Cambridge, in 1542, where he earned a bachelor's degree (1545) and a master's degree (1548); he also was made a fellow of Trinity College, Cambridge, on its founding in 1546. Dee furthered his scientific studies on the Continent with a short visit in 1547 and then a longer stay from 1548 to 1551 (both times to the Low Countries) under the mathematician-cartographers Pedro Nuñez, Gemma Frisius, Abraham Ortelius, and Gerardus Mercator; he also pursued his own studies in Paris and elsewhere. Dee turned down a mathematical professorship at the University of Paris in 1551 and a similar position at the University of Oxford in 1554, apparently in hopes of obtaining an official position with the English crown.

Following his return to England, Dee attached himself to the royal court, offering instruction in the mathematical sciences to both courtiers and navigators. He also served as consultant and astrologer to, among others, Queen Mary I. The latter activity landed him in jail in 1555 on the charge of being a conjurer, but he was soon released. Following the ascension of Elizabeth I to the throne in 1558, Dee became a scientific and medical adviser to the queen, and by the mid-1560s he established himself at Mortlake, near London. There he built a laboratory and amassed the largest private library in England at the time, which was said to number more than 4,000 books and manuscripts. He was as generous in making his library accessible to scholars as he was in assisting numerous practitioners who applied for advice.

Dee was intimately involved in laying the groundwork for several English voyages of exploration, instructing captains and pilots in the principles of mathematical navigation, preparing maps for their use, and furnishing them with various navigational instruments. He is most closely associated with the expeditions to Canada led by Sir Martin Frobisher in 1576–78 and with discussions in 1583 regarding a proposed but never commissioned search for the Northwest Passage. He was also active in publicly advocating a British empire, being the first to use that description in *General and Rare Memorials Pertayning to the Perfect Arte of Navigation* (1577). In 1582 Dee also recommended that England adopt the Gregorian calendar, but at that time the Anglican church refused to embrace such a "popish" innovation.

Dee's scientific interests were far broader than his involvement in English exploration might suggest.

In 1558 he published *Propaedeumata Aphoristica* ("An Aphoristic Introduction"), which presented his views on natural philosophy and astrology. Dee continued to discuss his occult views in 1564 with the *Monas hieroglyphica* (*The Hieroglyphic Monad* [2000]), wherein he offered a single mathematical-magical symbol as the key to unlocking the unity of nature. In addition to editing the first English translation of Euclid's *Elements* (1570), Dee added an influential preface that offered a powerful manifesto on the dignity and usefulness of the mathematical sciences. Furthermore, as passionately as he believed in the utility of mathematics for mundane matters, Dee expressed conviction in the occult power of mathematics to reveal divine mysteries.

Perhaps frustrated by his failure to arrive at a comprehensive understanding of natural knowledge, Dee sought divine assistance by attempting to converse with angels. He and his medium, the convicted counterfeiter Edward Kelley, held numerous séances both in England and on the Continent, where the two traveled together—mainly in Poland and Bohemia (now the Czech Republic)—between 1583 and 1589. By all accounts Dee was sincere, which is more than can be said for Kelley, who may have duped him. On Dee's return to England, his friends raised money for him and interceded on his behalf with Queen Elizabeth I. Though she appointed him warden of Manchester College in 1596, Dee's final years were marked by poverty and isolation. He was long said to have died at Mortlake in December 1608 and to have been buried in the Anglican church there, but there is evidence that his death occurred the following March at the London home of his acquaintance (and possible executor) John Pontois.

It is almost certain that William Shakespeare (1564–1616) modeled the character of Prospero in *The Tempest* (1611) on the career of John Dee, the Elizabethan magus.

Sir John Hawkins

(b. 1532, Plymouth, Devon, England—
d. November 12, 1595, at sea off Puerto Rico)

The English naval administrator and commander Sir John Hawkins (or Hawkyns) was one of the foremost seamen of 16th-century England and the chief architect of the Elizabethan navy.

A kinsman of Sir Francis Drake, Hawkins began his career as a merchant in the African trade and soon became the first English slave trader. By carrying slaves from Guinea, in West Africa, to the Spanish West Indies, he provoked conflict with the Spaniards, who did not allow unauthorized foreigners to trade with their colonies. Hawkins' first slave-trading voyage, in 1562–63, on behalf of a syndicate of London merchants, was so profitable that a more prestigious group, including Queen Elizabeth I, provided the money for a second expedition (1564–65). His third voyage, with Drake in 1567–69, however, ended in disaster. After selling the slaves in the Caribbean, Hawkins was forced by needed repairs and lack of water to take refuge at San Juan de Ulua, near Veracruz, Mexico. A Spanish fleet attacked him in the harbour, and, of the six ships, only the two commanded by Hawkins and Drake were able to escape. This episode marked the beginning of the long quarrel between England and Spain that eventually led to open war in 1585 and the defeat of the Spanish Armada three years later.

Hawkins soon avenged himself; by gaining the confidence of Spain's ambassador to England, he learned the

British ships being attacked by a Spanish fleet at San Juan de Ulua. Although the British were badly defeated, John Hawkins and his kinsman, Francis Drake, managed to escape. Hulton Archive/Getty Images

details of a conspiracy (the so-called Ridolfi plot of 1571) in which English Roman Catholics, with Spanish assistance, were to depose Queen Elizabeth and install Mary Stuart, Queen of Scots, on the English throne. Hawkins notified his government, and the English plotters involved were arrested.

In 1577 Hawkins succeeded his father-in-law, Benjamin Gonson, as treasurer of the navy; later (1589) he was to assume the additional duties of controller. His high naval post enabled him to direct the rebuilding of the older galleons and to contribute to the design of faster, more heavily armed ships. It was this new, swift-sailing navy that withstood the Spanish in 1588. Hawkins was third in command during the Armada crisis (during which he was knighted), and afterward he devised the strategy—quite original for that period—of setting up a naval blockade at the Azores to intercept Spanish treasure ships returning from the New World.

In 1595 Hawkins and Drake sailed with 27 ships to raid the Spanish West Indies. Hawkins died the night before an unsuccessful attack on Puerto Rico.

Sir Martin Frobisher

(b. c. 1535, Yorkshire, England—
d. November 22, 1594, Plymouth, Devon)

The English navigator, privateer, and adventurer Sir Martin Frobisher was an early explorer of Canada's northeast coast. Frobisher went on voyages to the Guinea coast of Africa in 1553 and 1554, and during the 1560s he preyed on French shipping in the English Channel under a privateering license from the English crown; he was arrested several times on charges of piracy but never brought to trial.

Having become interested in the possibility of finding a Northwest Passage from the Atlantic Ocean to the Pacific Ocean, Frobisher in 1576 obtained the command of three small ships, in one of which he succeeded in crossing the Atlantic that year. He reached Labrador and Baffin Island and discovered the bay that now bears his name. He returned to England with reports of possible gold mines, thereby obtaining royal backing for two further expeditions to the same area, in 1577 and 1578. On the latter of these expeditions, Frobisher sailed up Hudson Strait but then turned back to anchor at Frobisher Bay, where his attempts to establish a colony were unsuccessful. Frobisher's single-minded pursuit of mineral treasure limited the exploratory value of his voyages, and, when the ores he brought back from his third voyage proved to contain neither silver nor gold, his financing collapsed, and he was forced to seek other employment.

In 1585 Frobisher sailed as vice admiral of Sir Francis Drake's expedition to the West Indies, and three years later he played a prominent part in the campaign that defeated the Spanish Armada, being knighted during the operations. Over the next six years Frobisher commanded various English naval squadrons, including one in the Azores (1591) that unsuccessfully sought to capture Spanish treasure ships. In 1594 he was mortally wounded fighting a Spanish force on the west coast of France. Frobisher was undoubtedly one of the ablest seamen of his time, but as an explorer he lacked the capacity for patient factual investigation.

Sir Humphrey Gilbert

(b. c. 1539—d. September 1583, at sea near the Azores)

Sir Humphrey Gilbert was an English soldier and navigator who devised daring and farseeing projects of overseas colonization. Although he was brilliant and creative, his poor leadership was responsible for his failure to establish the first permanent English colony in North America. He succeeded, however, in annexing Newfoundland.

The half brother of Sir Walter Raleigh and a cousin of Sir Richard Grenville, Gilbert studied navigation and military science at the University of Oxford, entered the army, and was wounded at the siege of Le Havre (1563). In 1566 he wrote a *Discourse* proposing a voyage in search of a Northwest Passage between the Atlantic and Pacific oceans via North America. But Queen Elizabeth I rejected the idea and instead sent Gilbert to Ireland (1567–70), where he ruthlessly suppressed an uprising and began to elaborate plans for a Protestant colonization of the province of Munster, in southern Ireland. He was knighted for this action in 1570. In 1572 he commanded a group of 1,500 English volunteers sent to assist the revolt of the Netherlands against Spain.

By the mid-1570s Gilbert had begun to apply his Irish colonization schemes to North America. In 1577 he put forth a plan for seizing the Newfoundland fishing fleets of Spain, Portugal, and France; occupying Santo Domingo and Cuba; and intercepting the ships carrying American silver to Spain. The queen ignored his proposal but in 1578 granted him a six-year charter to settle "heathen lands not actually possessed of any Christian prince or people."

Straining his means to the utmost, Gilbert finally outfitted a seven-ship expedition and set sail on November 19, 1578. He probably intended to cross to North America, but his ill-equipped, badly disciplined force quickly broke up, and by the spring of 1579 some of the ships had drifted to England while others had turned to piracy. During the summer of 1579 Gilbert helped put down the rebellion of James Fitzgerald (called Fitzmaurice) in Ireland.

Gilbert then set about organizing a more ambitious colonizing expedition. He sailed from Plymouth on June 11, 1583, and on August 3 arrived at the vicinity of what is now St. John's, Newfoundland, which he claimed in the name of the queen. Moving southward with three ships, he lost the largest of them on August 29 and two days later turned homeward. He was last seen during a great storm in the Atlantic, shouting to his companion vessel, "We are as near heaven by sea as by land." Gilbert's ship was then swallowed by the sea.

SIR FRANCIS DRAKE

(b. 1540–43, Devonshire, England—
d. January 28, 1596, at sea off Puerto Bello
[now Portobelo], Panama)

English adventurer, privateer, and admiral Sir Francis Drake led the second circumnavigation of the globe (1577–80) and was the most renowned seaman of the Elizabethan Age.

EARLY LIFE

Born on the Crowndale estate of Lord Francis Russell, 2nd earl of Bedford, Drake's father, Edmund Drake, was the son of one of Russell's tenant farmers. Edmund fled his native county after he was arraigned for assault and

Francis Drake. Epics/Hulton Fine Art Collection/Getty Images

robbery in 1548. The claim that he was a refugee from Roman Catholic persecution was a later pious fiction. From even before his father's departure, Francis was brought up among relatives in Plymouth: the Hawkins family (including John Hawkins), who combined vocations as merchants and pirates.

When Drake was about 18, he enlisted in the Hawkins family fleet, which prowled for shipping to plunder or seize off the French coast. By the early 1560s, he had graduated to the African trade, in which the Hawkins family had an increasing interest, and by 1568 he had command of his own ship on a Hawkins venture of illicit slave-trading in the Spanish colonies of the Caribbean.

VOYAGES TO THE WEST INDIES

Resenting the Spanish authorities' claims to regulate their colonies' trade and impound contraband, Drake later referred to some "wrongs" that he and his companions had suffered—wrongs that he was determined to right in the years to come. His second voyage to the West Indies, in company with John Hawkins, ended disastrously at San Juan de Ulúa off the coast of Mexico, when the English interlopers were attacked by the Spanish and many of them killed. Drake escaped during the attack and returned to England in command of a small vessel, the *Judith*, with an even greater determination to have his revenge upon Spain and the Spanish king, Philip II. Although the expedition was a financial failure, it brought Drake to the attention of Queen Elizabeth I, who had herself invested in the slave-trading venture. In the years that followed, he made two expeditions in small vessels to the West Indies, in order "to gain such intelligence as might further him to get some amend for his loss." In 1572—having obtained from the queen a privateering commission, which amounted to a license to plunder in the king of Spain's lands—Drake set sail for America in command of two small ships, the 70-ton *Pasha* and the 25-ton *Swan*. He was nothing if not ambitious, for his aim was to capture the important town of Nombre de Dios, Panama. Although Drake was wounded in the attack, which failed, he and his men managed to get away with a great deal of plunder by successfully attacking a silver-bearing mule train. This was perhaps the foundation of Drake's fortune. In the interval between these episodes, he crossed the Isthmus of Panama. Standing on a high ridge of land, he first saw the Pacific, that ocean hitherto barred to all but Spanish ships. It was then, as he put it, that he "besought Almighty God of His goodness to give him life and leave to sail once in an English ship in that sea." He returned to England both rich and famous. Unfortunately, his return coincided with a moment when Queen Elizabeth and King Philip II of Spain had reached a temporary truce. Although delighted with Drake's success in the empire of her great enemy, Elizabeth could not officially acknowledge piracy. Drake saw that the time was inauspicious and sailed with a small squadron to Ireland, where he served under the earl of Essex and took part in a notorious massacre in July 1575. An obscure period of Drake's life follows; he makes almost no appearance in the records until 1577.

CIRCUMNAVIGATION OF THE WORLD

In 1577 he was chosen as the leader of an expedition intended to pass around South America through the Strait of Magellan and to explore the coast that lay beyond. The

EXPLORERS OF THE LATE RENAISSANCE AND THE ENLIGHTENMENT: FROM SIR FRANCIS DRAKE TO MUNGO PARK

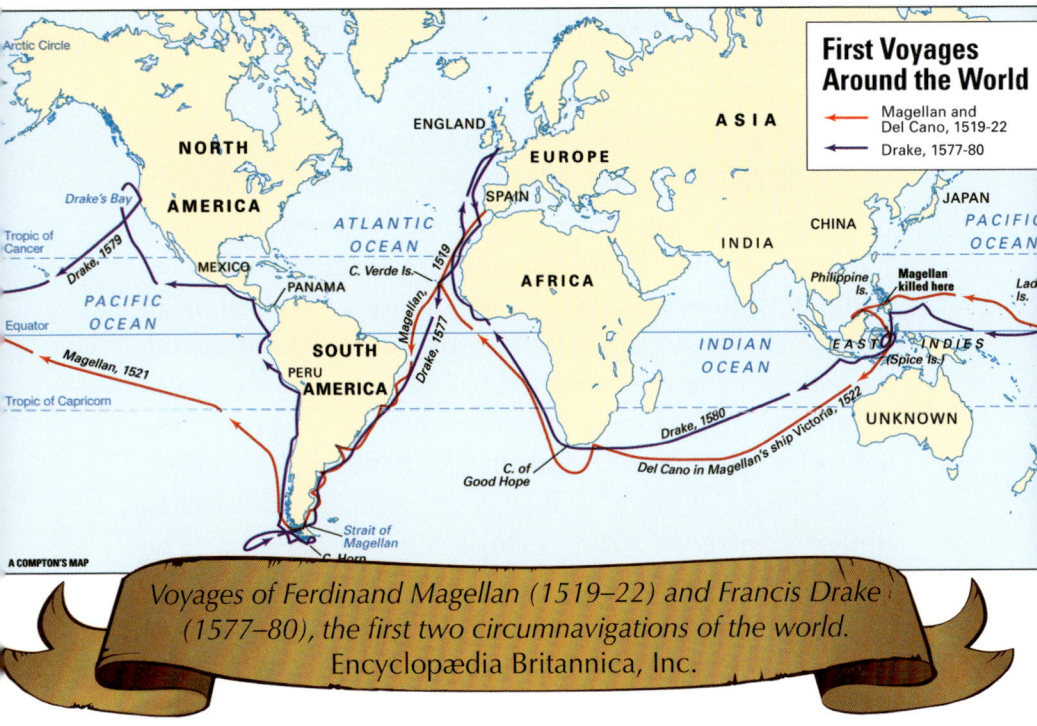

Voyages of Ferdinand Magellan (1519–22) and Francis Drake (1577–80), the first two circumnavigations of the world. Encyclopædia Britannica, Inc.

expedition was backed by the queen herself. Nothing could have suited Drake better. He had official approval to benefit himself and the queen, as well as to cause the maximum damage to the Spaniards. This was the occasion on which he first met the queen face-to-face and heard from her own lips that she "would gladly be revenged on the king of Spain for divers injuries that I have received." The explicit object was to "find out places meet to have traffic." Drake, however, devoted the voyage to piracy, without official reproof in England. He set sail in December with five small ships, manned by fewer than 200 men, and reached the Brazilian coast in the spring of 1578. His flagship, the *Pelican*, which Drake later renamed the *Golden Hind* (or *Hinde*), weighed only about 100 tons. It seemed little enough with which to undertake a venture into the domain of what was then the most powerful monarch and empire in the world.

Upon arrival in South America, Drake alleged a plot by unreliable officers, and its supposed leader, Thomas Doughty, was tried and executed. Drake was always a stern disciplinarian, and he clearly did not intend to continue the venture without making sure that all of his small company were loyal to him. Two of his smaller vessels, having served their purpose as store ships, were then abandoned after their provisions had been taken aboard the others, and on August 21, 1578, he entered the Strait of Magellan. It took 16 days to sail through, after which Drake had his second view of the Pacific Ocean—this time from the deck of an English ship. Then, as he wrote, "God by a contrary wind and intolerable tempest seemed to set himself against us." During the gale, Drake's vessel and that of his second in command had been separated; the latter, having missed a rendezvous with Drake, ultimately returned to England, presuming that the *Hind* had sunk. It was, therefore, only Drake's flagship that made its way into the Pacific and up the coast of South America. He passed along the coast like a whirlwind, for the Spaniards were quite unguarded, having never known a hostile ship in their waters. He seized provisions at Valparaíso, attacked passing Spanish merchantmen, and captured two very rich prizes that were carrying bars of gold and silver, minted Spanish coinage, precious stones, and pearls. He claimed then to have sailed to the north as far as 48° N, on a parallel with Vancouver [Canada], to seek the Northwest Passage back into the Atlantic. Bitterly cold weather defeated him, and he coasted southward to anchor near what is now San Francisco. He named the surrounding country New Albion and took possession of it in the name of Queen Elizabeth.

EXPLORERS OF THE LATE RENAISSANCE AND THE ENLIGHTENMENT: FROM SIR FRANCIS DRAKE TO MUNGO PARK

In July 1579 he sailed west across the Pacific and after 68 days sighted a line of islands (probably the remote Palau group). From there he went on to the Philippines, where he watered ship before sailing to the Moluccas. There he was well received by a local sultan and succeeded in buying spices. Drake's deep-sea navigation and pilotage were always excellent, but in those totally uncharted waters his

Two cross-section views of the Golden Hind, *the ship in which Francis Drake circumnavigated the world.* DEA Picture Library/De Agostini/Getty Images

ship struck a reef. He was able to get her off without any great damage and, after calling at Java, set his course across the Indian Ocean for the Cape of Good Hope. Two years after she had nosed her way into the Strait of Magellan, the *Golden Hind* came back into the Atlantic with only 56 of the original crew of 100 left aboard.

On September 26, 1580, Francis Drake took his ship into Plymouth Harbour. She was laden with treasure and spices, and Drake's fortune was permanently made. Despite Spanish protests about his piratical conduct while in their imperial waters, Queen Elizabeth herself went aboard the *Golden Hind*, which was lying at Deptford in the Thames estuary, and personally bestowed knighthood on him.

MAYOR OF PLYMOUTH

In the same year, 1581, Drake was made mayor of Plymouth, an office he fulfilled with the same thoroughness that he had shown in all other matters. He organized a water supply for Plymouth that served the city for 300 years. Drake's first wife, a Cornish woman named Mary Newman, whom he had married in 1569, died in 1583, and in 1585 he married again. His second wife, Elizabeth Sydenham, was an heiress and the daughter of a local Devonshire magnate, Sir George Sydenham. In keeping with his new station, Drake purchased a fine country house—Buckland Abbey (now a national museum)—a few miles from Plymouth. Drake's only grief was that neither of his wives bore him any children.

During these years of fame when Drake was a popular hero, he could always obtain volunteers for any of his expeditions. But he was very differently regarded by many of his great contemporaries. Such well-born men as the naval commander Sir Richard Grenville and the navigator and explorer Sir Martin Frobisher disliked him intensely. He was the parvenu, the rich but common upstart, with West Country manners and accent and with none of the courtier's graces. Drake had even bought Buckland Abbey from the Grenvilles by a ruse, using an intermediary, for he knew that the Grenvilles would never have sold it to him directly. It is doubtful, in any case, whether he cared about their opinions, so long as he retained the goodwill of the queen. This was soon enough demonstrated when in 1585 Elizabeth placed him in command of a fleet of 25 ships. Hostilities with Spain had broken out once more, and he was ordered to cause as much damage as possible to the Spaniards' overseas empire. Drake fulfilled his commission, capturing Santiago in the Cape Verde Islands and taking and plundering the cities of Cartagena in Colombia, St. Augustine in Florida, and San Domingo (now Santo Domingo, Dominican Republic). Lord Burghley, Elizabeth's principal minister, who had never approved of Drake or his methods, was forced to concede that "Sir Francis Drake is a fearful man to the king of Spain."

FAILURE OF THE SPANISH ARMADA

By 1586 it was known that Philip II was preparing a fleet for what was called "The Enterprise of England" and that he had the blessing of Pope Sixtus V to return the English crown—Protestant since Henry VIII—to the fold of Rome. Drake was given carte blanche by the queen to "impeach the provisions of Spain." In the following year, with a fleet of some 30 ships, he showed that her trust in him had not been misplaced. He stormed into the Spanish harbour of Cádiz and in 36 hours destroyed numerous vessels and thousands of tons of supplies, all of which had been destined for the Armada. This action, which he laughingly referred to as "singeing the king of Spain's beard," helped to delay the invasion fleet for a further year. But the resources of Spain were such that by July 1588 the Armada was in the English Channel. Lord Howard had been chosen as English admiral to oppose it. Drake appropriated a prize—a Spanish galleon disabled in an accidental collision—but, although credited by legend with a heroic role, is not known to have played any part in the fighting.

LAST YEARS

Drake's later years, however, were not happy. An expedition that he led to Portugal proved abortive, and his last voyage, in 1596 against the Spanish possessions in the West Indies, was a failure, largely because the fleet was decimated by a fever to which Drake himself succumbed. He was buried at sea off the town of Puerto Bello (modern Portobelo, Panama). As the Elizabethan historian John Stow wrote:

> *He was more skilful in all points of navigation than any….He was also of a perfect memory, great observation, eloquent by nature….In brief he was as famous in Europe and America, as Timur Lenk [Tamerlane] in Asia and Africa.*

At home his reputation was equivocal. Fellow captains found him unreliable and self-seeking. His Spanish victims, however, conceded grudging admiration: he was credited with diabolical powers as a navigator and became the antihero of works of literature, in which he was celebrated for courtesy to prisoners. But to the Spaniards he was also, as their ambassador to England remarked, "the master-thief of the unknown world." He was "low of stature, of strong limb, round-headed, brown hair, full-bearded, his eyes round, large and clear, well-favoured face and of a cheerful countenance." His life was dedicated to self-aggrandizement and revenge directed at Spain. But his legend influenced English self-perceptions, for he was credited with feats of sangfroid, unflappability, improvisation, tenacity, and fair play, most of which have little or no basis in fact.

Willem Barents

(b. c. 1550—d. June 20, 1597, the Arctic)

Willem Barents was a Dutch navigator who searched for a Northeast Passage from Europe to Asia and for whom the Barents Sea was named. Because of his extensive voyages, accurate charting, and the valuable meteorological data he collected, he is regarded as one of the most important early Arctic explorers.

In 1594 he left Amsterdam with two ships and reached the west coast of Novaya Zemlya, which he followed northward until forced to turn back near its northern extremity. In the following year he commanded another expedition, of seven ships, which made for the strait between the Asian coast and Vaygach Island but was too late to find open water. On a third voyage (1596), he sighted Spitsbergen (now Svalbard), but upon rounding the north of Novaya Zemlya his ship became trapped in ice, and Barents was compelled to winter in the north. He lived only a week after he and his party were able to leave in open boats. The Arctic dwelling in which the party had wintered was found in 1871; many of its relics are preserved at The Hague, Netherlands. In 1875 a portion of his journal was found.

John Davis

(b. c. 1550, Sandridge, near Dartmouth, Devon, England—d. December 29/30, 1605, off Bintan Island, near Singapore)

English navigator and explorer John Davis (or Davys) attempted to find the Northwest Passage through the Canadian Arctic to the Pacific. He appears to have first proposed his plan to look for the Northwest Passage in 1583 to Sir Francis Walsingham, principal secretary to Queen Elizabeth I. In 1585 he began his first northwestern expedition. Coming upon the icebound east shore of Greenland, he headed south, rounded Cape Farewell, and then sailed northward along the coast of western Greenland. Turning in what he thought was the direction of China, he sailed some distance up Cumberland Sound, which cuts into Baffin Island, but eventually turned back.

He attempted to find the Northwest Passage again in 1586 and in 1587. On the last of these voyages he passed through the strait named for him, entered Baffin Bay, and coasted northward along western Greenland to Disko Island, about latitude 70° N. Davis showed some imagination in his dealings with the Greenland Inuit (Eskimos). He took musicians with him and had his sailors dance to the music, which helped to establish cordial relations with the local peoples. Cape Walsingham and Cumberland Sound are among the many Arctic points that he named.

Davis seems to have commanded the Black Dog against the Spanish Armada (1588) and sailed with Thomas Cavendish on his last voyage (1591). In seeking a passage through the Strait of Magellan, Davis discovered the Falkland Islands (August 9, 1592). He sailed with Sir Walter Raleigh to Cádiz and to the Azores (1596–97) and accompanied expeditions to the East Indies in 1598 and 1601. On a third voyage to the Indies he was killed by Japanese pirates.

Davis invented a device (called the backstaff, or Davis quadrant) used until the 18th century for determining latitude by reading the angle of elevation of the sun, and he wrote a treatise on navigation, The Seaman's Secret (1594). His work The World's Hydrographical Description (1595) deals with the Northwest Passage.

Sir Walter Raleigh

(b. 1554?, Hayes Barton, near Budleigh Salterton, Devon, England—d. October 29, 1618, London)

English adventurer and writer Sir Walter Raleigh (or Ralegh) was a favourite of Queen Elizabeth I, who knighted him in 1585. Accused of treason by Elizabeth's successor, James I, he was imprisoned in the Tower of London and eventually put to death.

Raleigh was a younger son of Walter Raleigh (d. 1581) of Fardell in Devon, by his third wife, Katherine Gilbert (née Champernowne). In 1569 he fought on the Huguenot (French Protestant) side in the Wars of Religion in France, and he is known later to have been at Oriel College, Oxford (1572), and at the Middle Temple law college (1575). In 1580 he fought against the Irish rebels in Munster, and his outspoken criticism of the way English policy was being implemented in Ireland brought him to the attention of Queen Elizabeth. By 1582 he had become the monarch's favourite, and he began to acquire lucrative monopolies, properties, and influential positions. His Irish service was rewarded by vast estates in Munster. In 1583 the queen secured him a lease of part of Durham House in the Strand, London, where he had a monopoly of wine licenses (1583) and of the export of broadcloth (1585); and he became warden of the stannaries (the Cornish tin mines), lieutenant of Cornwall, and vice admiral of Devon and Cornwall and frequently sat as a member of Parliament. In 1587, two years after he had been knighted, Raleigh became captain of the queen's guard. His last appointment under the crown was as governor of Jersey (one of the Channel Islands) in 1600.

In 1592 Raleigh acquired the manor of Sherborne in Dorset. He wanted to settle and found a family. His marriage to Elizabeth, daughter of Sir Nicholas Throckmorton, possibly as early as 1588, had been kept a secret from the jealous queen. In 1592 the birth of a son betrayed him, and he and his wife were both imprisoned in the Tower of London. Raleigh bought his release with profits from a privateering voyage in which he had invested, but he never regained his ascendancy at court. The child did not

Walter Raleigh laying his cloak across a puddle for Queen Elizabeth I. Hulton Archive/Getty Images

survive; a second son, Walter, was born in 1593 and a third son, Carew, in 1604 or 1605.

Although Raleigh was the queen's favourite, he was not popular. His pride and extravagant spending were notorious, and he was attacked for unorthodox thought. A Jesuit pamphlet in 1592 accused him of keeping a "School of Atheism," but he was not an atheist in the modern sense. He was a bold talker, interested in skeptical philosophy, and a serious student of mathematics as an aid to navigation. He also studied chemistry and compounded medical formulas.

Raleigh's breach with the queen widened his personal sphere of action. Between 1584 and 1589 he had tried to establish a colony near Roanoke Island (in present North Carolina), which he named Virginia, but he never set foot there himself. In 1595 he led an expedition to what is now Venezuela, in South America, sailing up the Orinoco River in the heart of Spain's colonial empire. He described the expedition in his book *The Discoverie of Guiana* (1596). Spanish documents and stories told by Indians had convinced him of the existence of Eldorado (El Dorado), the ruler of Manoa, a supposedly fabulous city of gold in the interior of South America. He did locate some gold mines, but no one supported his project for colonizing the area. In 1596 he went with Robert Devereux, 2nd earl of Essex, on an unsuccessful expedition to the Spanish city of Cádiz, and he was Essex's rear admiral on the Islands voyage in 1597, an expedition to the Azores.

Raleigh's aggressive policies toward Spain did not recommend him to the pacific King James I (reigned 1603–25). His enemies worked to bring about his ruin, and in 1603 he and others were accused of plotting to dethrone the king. Raleigh was convicted on the written evidence of Henry Brooke, Lord Cobham, and, after a last-minute reprieve from the death sentence, was consigned to the Tower. He fought to save Sherborne, which he had conveyed in trust for his son, but a clerical error invalidated the deed. In 1616 he was released but not pardoned. He still hoped to exploit the wealth of Venezuela, arguing that the country had been ceded to England by its native chiefs in 1595. With the king's permission, he financed and led a second expedition there, promising to open a gold mine without offending Spain. A severe fever prevented his leading his men upriver. His lieutenant, Lawrence Kemys, burned a Spanish settlement but found no gold. Raleigh's son Walter died in the action. King James invoked the suspended sentence of 1603, and in 1618, after writing a spirited defense of his acts, Raleigh was executed.

Popular feeling had been on Raleigh's side ever since 1603. After 1618 his occasional writings were collected and published, often with little discrimination. The authenticity of some minor works attributed to him is still unsure. Some 560 lines of verse in his hand are preserved. They address the queen as Cynthia and complain of her unkindness, probably with reference to his imprisonment of 1592. His best-known prose works in addition to *The Discoverie of Guiana* are *A Report of the Truth of the Fight About the Iles of Açores This Last Sommer* (1591; generally known as *The Last Fight of the Revenge*) and *The History of the World* (1614). The last work, undertaken in the Tower, proceeds from the Creation to the 2nd century BCE. History is shown as a record of God's Providence, a doctrine that pleased contemporaries and counteracted the charge of atheism. King James was meant to note the many warnings that the injustice of kings is always punished.

Raleigh survives as an interesting and enigmatic personality rather than as a force in history. He can be presented either as a hero or as a scoundrel. His vaulting imagination, which could envisage both North and South

America as English territory, was supported by considerable practical ability and a persuasive pen, but some discrepancy between the vision and the deed made him less effective than his gifts had promised.

Thomas Cavendish

(baptized September 19, 1560, Trimley St. Martin, Suffolk, England—d. *c.* May 1592, in the North Atlantic)

The English navigator, adventurer, and freebooter Thomas Cavendish (or Candish) was the leader of the third circumnavigation of Earth.

Cavendish accompanied Sir Richard Grenville on his voyage to America (1585) and, upon returning to England, undertook an elaborate imitation of Sir Francis Drake's circumnavigation. On July 21, 1586, he sailed from Plymouth with 123 men in three vessels. He reached the Patagonian coast of South America, where he discovered Port Desire (now Puerto Deseado, Argentina), his only significant contribution to geographical knowledge. After passing through the Strait of Magellan, he attacked Spanish settlements and shipping from South America to Mexico. Among his prizes was the treasure galleon *Santa Ana*, seized off the coast of California (November 14, 1587). After touching the Philippines, the Moluccas, and Java, his expedition rounded the Cape of Good Hope and arrived at Plymouth on September 9/10, 1588, with only one of his ships, the *Desire*, and much plunder. On his second American-Pacific venture, undertaken in 1591, his fleet failed to traverse the Strait of Magellan, and Cavendish died trying to get back to England.

SIR RICHARD HAWKINS

(b. c. 1560—d. April 18, 1622, London, England)

Sir Richard Hawkins (or Hawkyns) was an English seaman and adventurer whose *Observations in His Voyage Into the South Sea* (1622) gives the best extant idea of Elizabethan life at sea and was used by Charles Kingsley for his adventure novel *Westward Ho!* (1855).

The only son of the famed seaman Sir John Hawkins by his first marriage, Richard Hawkins in 1582 sailed with his uncle William to the West Indies; in 1585 he commanded a ship on Sir Francis Drake's raid on the Spanish Main and was a ship captain during the Armada campaign (1588).

In June 1593 he sailed from Plymouth in the *Dainty* with two smaller vessels, which parted company before reaching the Pacific Ocean. In February 1594 he sighted what he called Hawkins Maidenland, probably the Falkland Islands, which had been discovered two years previously by John Davis. After burning four ships at Valparaíso (now in Chile), Hawkins continued up the South American coast until he met six Spanish warships off Callao (Peru), near Lima. He overcame them; but on June 22, when north of Paita (also Peru), he was wounded and forced to surrender after a fight lasting three days with two more Spanish ships. He was imprisoned at Lima and then from 1597 till 1602 in Spain, at which date his ransom of £3,000 was paid. On his return he was knighted and elected mayor and MP for Plymouth. In 1608, after five years as vice-admiral of Devon, he was arrested and fined for condoning piracy. In 1620 he sailed as second in command of an ineffective expedition against the Algerine corsairs.

His *Observations in His Voyage Into the South Sea* was printed in 1622, having been composed about 1603.

William Adams

(b. 1564, Gillingham, Kent, England—d. May 26, 1620, Hirado, Japan)

The navigator and merchant-adventurer William Adams was the first Englishman to visit Japan.

At the age of 12 Adams was apprenticed to a shipbuilder in the merchant marine, and, in 1588, he was master of a supply ship for the British navy during the invasion of the Spanish Armada. Soon after the British victory, he began serving as pilot and ship's master for a company of Barbary merchants. In June 1598 he shipped out as pilot major with five Dutch ships bound from Europe for the East Indies (present-day Indonesia) via the Strait of Magellan. The trouble-ridden fleet was scattered by storms, and in April 1600

Adams's ship, the *Liefde* ("Charity"), its crew sick and dying, anchored off the island of Kyushu in southern Japan, the first northern European ship to reach that country.

Adams and other survivors were summoned to Ōsaka, where Tokugawa Ieyasu—soon to become the shogun (generalissimo) of Japan—interrogated mainly Adams about a variety of political, religious, and technological topics. Ieyasu was so impressed with Adams's knowledge, especially of ships and shipbuilding, that he made the Englishman one of his confidants. Adams was given the rank of *hatamoto* ("bannerman"), a retainer to the shogun, and was awarded an estate, Miura, on the Miura Peninsula south of Edo (now Tokyo). Despite those honours, in the early years of his sojourn Adams repeatedly expressed his desire to return to England (where he had a wife and family,

William Adams (centre, standing) *addressing Tokugawa Ieyasu.* Henry Guttmann/Hulton Archive/Getty Images

whom he eventually was able to continue to support) but was refused permission. He thus became permanently settled in Japan, married a Japanese woman, had a second family there, and came to be known by the name Anjin ("Pilot"; later called Miura Anjin).

Adams oversaw the construction of several Western-style ships, wrote letters on behalf of the shogun encouraging Dutch and English traders to come to Japan, and then officiated between the Tokugawa shogunate and the traders who began visiting the country. In 1613 he helped to establish an English factory (trading post) for the East India Company at Hirado, in Kyushu, northwest of Nagasaki. Adams was allowed to undertake several overseas voyages between 1614 and 1619; during those he piloted Japanese trading ships to destinations as far away as Okinawa and Southeast Asia.

Ieyasu died in 1616, however, and under his successor, Tokugawa Hidetada, Japan became increasingly isolationist. The activities of the English traders were curtailed (eventually the Dutch were the only Europeans allowed to trade with Japan), and Adams found his influence with the shogunate greatly diminished. By 1620 Adams was ill, and while in Hirado he died and was buried there. The English factory was shut down soon thereafter.

Adams's career in Japan was the inspiration for a number of English- as well as Japanese-language books, notably James Clavell's best-selling novel *Shogun* (1975), which was also the basis for a popular U.S. television miniseries of the same name (1980). In addition to his Miura estate, Adams had a house in Edo (now Tokyo), and the neighbourhood where it was located is still called Anjin-chō. Among the annual observances for him in Japan are those held in Hirado (May) and in Itō, Shizuoka prefecture (August), the latter commemorating the place where the first Western-style ships were built and launched.

Pedro Páez

(b. 1564, Olmedo, Spain—d. May 20, 1622, Gorgora, Ethiopia)

Pedro (or Pero) Páez Xaramillo was a learned Jesuit priest who, in the tradition of Frumentius—founder of the Ethiopian church—went as a missionary to Ethiopia, where he became known as the second apostle of Ethiopia.

Páez entered the Society of Jesus (Jesuits) in 1582 and sailed for Goa, in India, in 1588. En route to Ethiopia (1589) he was captured by Turkish pirates and enslaved until 1596, when he returned to Goa. He finally reached Ethiopia in 1603. There he learned two of the main languages, translated a catechism, and wrote a treatise on the theological errors of the Ethiopian church and a history of the country. He succeeded in converting some Ethiopians to Roman Catholicism. In 1618 he traced the source of the Blue Nile River to Lake Tana in the northern Ethiopian highlands.

Henry Hudson

(b. c. 1565, England—d. after June 22, 1611, in or near Hudson Bay?)

Henry Hudson was an English navigator and explorer who, sailing three times for the English (1607, 1608,

1610–11) and once for the Dutch (1609), tried to discover a short route from Europe to Asia through the Arctic Ocean, in both the Old World and the New. A river, a strait, and a bay in North America are named for him.

Of Hudson's early life, nothing is known. Several Hudsons were associated with his sponsors, the Muscovy Company of London, a generation before his own time. A 1585 voyage by the English navigator John Davis, who sailed to the Arctic to make the first attempt to find a Northwest Passage from Europe to Asia, was planned in the home of a Thomas Hudson in the Limehouse area of London's East End. Henry Hudson may have been present on that occasion and consequently developed a lifelong interest in Arctic exploration. It is certain that he was well informed about Arctic geography and that his competence as a navigator was such that two wealthy companies chose him to conduct hazardous explorations.

THE SEARCH FOR THE NORTHEAST PASSAGE

In the spring of 1607, sailing for the Muscovy Company, Hudson, his son John, and 10 companions set forth "for to discover a Passage by the North Pole to Japan and China." Believing that he would find an ice-free sea around the North Pole, Hudson struck out northward. On reaching the edge of the polar ice pack, he followed it east until he reached the Svalbard (Spitsbergen) archipelago. From there he extended explorations made earlier by the 16th-century Dutch navigator Willem Barents, who had also sought a Northeast Passage to Asia.

A year later, the Muscovy Company again sent Hudson to seek a Northeast Passage, this time between Svalbard

EXPLORERS OF THE LATE RENAISSANCE AND THE ENLIGHTENMENT: FROM SIR FRANCIS DRAKE TO MUNGO PARK

Full-scale replica of Henry Hudson's sailing ship Half Moon *in New York Harbor, 1909.* Library of Congress, Washington, D.C. (digital. id. cph 3b19440)

and the islands of Novaya Zemlya, which lie to the east of the Barents Sea. Finding his way again blocked by ice fields, he returned to England.

Shortly after his return, Hudson was lured to Amsterdam to undertake a third northeast voyage under contract to the Dutch East India Company. While there, he heard reports of two possible channels to the Pacific across North America. One of these, said to be in about latitude 62° N, was described in the logbooks of a voyage made in 1602 by an English explorer, Captain George Weymouth. The other, said to be in the vicinity of about latitude 40° N, was newly reported from Virginia by the English soldier, explorer, and colonist Captain John Smith. Although his interest in a Northwest Passage had been aroused, Hudson agreed to return directly to Holland if his northeast voyage should prove unsuccessful.

Hudson sailed from Holland in the *Half Moon* on April 6, 1609. When head winds and storms forced him to abandon his northeast voyage, he ignored his agreement and proposed to the crew that they should instead seek the Northwest Passage. Given their choice between returning home or continuing, the crew elected to follow up Smith's suggestion and seek the Northwest Passage around 40° N. While cruising along the Atlantic seaboard, Hudson put into the majestic river encountered by the Florentine navigator Giovanni da Verrazano in 1524, which was thenceforth to be known as the Hudson. After ascending it for about 150 miles (240 km) to the vicinity of what is now Albany, New York, Hudson concluded that the river did not lead to the Pacific.

On his way to Holland, Hudson docked at Dartmouth, England. The English government then ordered him and the English members of his crew to desist from further explorations for other nations. His log and papers were sent to Holland, where his discoveries were soon made known.

Hudson now made ready a voyage to America to follow up Weymouth's suggestion. Weymouth had described an inlet (now Hudson Strait) where a "furious overfall" of water rushed out with every ebb tide. This phenomenon suggested that a great body of water lay beyond the strait. Hudson was confident that it was the Pacific Ocean. The British East India Company contributed £300 toward his voyage, and the Muscovy Company presumably furnished a like amount; Hudson's private sponsors included 5 noblemen and 13 merchants.

THE VOYAGE TO HUDSON BAY

Sailing from London on April 17, 1610, in the 55-ton vessel *Discovery*, Hudson stopped briefly in Iceland, then proceeded to the "furious overfall." Passing through it and entering Hudson Bay, he then followed the east coast southward, rather than striking boldly westward. Finding himself in James Bay at the southernmost extremity of Hudson Bay and with no outlet to the Pacific to be found, Hudson cruised aimlessly until winter overtook him.

In the close confinement of an Arctic winter, quarrels arose. Hudson angered one of his crew, Henry Green, by first giving him a gray gown and then, when Green displeased him, taking it back and giving it to another. Some of his crew suspected that Hudson was secretly hoarding food for his favourites, and tempers flared when Hudson ordered the crew's own sea chests searched for extra victuals. Robert Juet, the mate, had been demoted, and he conspired with Green and others to mutiny. Once the homeward voyage had begun, the mutineers seized Hudson, his son, and seven others, casting them adrift in Hudson Bay in a small open boat on June 22, 1611. Although the *Discovery* sailed home to England, neither of the ringleaders returned with her, having been killed, together with several others, in a fight with Inuit (Eskimos). No more was ever heard of Hudson and his small party, although in 1631 to 1632 another explorer

Henry Hudson being abandoned by the crew of the Discovery *in Hudson Bay, Canada, on June 22, 1611; lithograph by Lewis & Browne, Library of Congress, Washington, D.C. Library of Congress, Washington, D.C.*

found the ruins of a shelter, possibly erected by the castaways.

As a commander, Hudson was more headstrong than courageous. He violated his agreement with the Dutch and failed to suppress the 1611 mutiny. He played favourites and let morale suffer. In James Bay he appeared irresolute.

Yet Hudson undertook four dangerous voyages, brought his crew through an Arctic winter, and preserved his vessels amid the dangers of ice and unknown shores. He was a competent navigator who materially extended the explorations of Verrazano, Davis, and Barents. His contribution to geographical knowledge was great, while his discoveries formed the basis for the Dutch colonization of the Hudson River and for English claims to much of Canada.

Samuel de Champlain

(b. 1567, Brouage, France—
d. December 25, 1635, Quebec, New France
[now in Quebec, Canada])

The French explorer and colonist Samuel de Champlain was the acknowledged founder of the city of Quebec (1608) and the consolidator of the French colonies in the

Samuel de Champlain. Encyclopædia Britannica, Inc.

New World. He was the European discoverer of the lake that bears his name (1609) and made other explorations of what are now northern New York, the Ottawa River basin, and the eastern Great Lakes.

Champlain was probably born a commoner, but, after acquiring a reputation as a navigator (having taken part in an expedition to the West Indies and Central America), he received an honorary if unofficial title at the court of Henry IV. In 1603 he accepted an invitation to visit what he called the River of Canada (St. Lawrence River). He sailed, as an observer in a longboat, upstream from the mother ship's anchorage at Tadoussac, a summer trading post, to the site of Montreal and its rapids. His report on the expedition was soon published in France, and in 1604 he accompanied a group of ill-fated settlers to Acadia, a region surrounding the Bay of Fundy.

Champlain spent three winters in Acadia—the first on an island in the St. Croix River, where scurvy killed nearly half the party, and the second and third, which claimed the lives of fewer men, at Annapolis Basin. During the summers he searched for an ideal site for colonization. His explorations led him down the Atlantic coast southward to Massachusetts Bay and beyond, mapping in detail the harbours that his English rivals had only touched. In 1607 the English came to Kennebec (now in Maine) in southern Acadia. They spent only one winter there, but the threat of conflict increased French interest in colonization.

Heading an expedition that left France in 1608, Champlain undertook his most ambitious project—the founding of Quebec. On earlier expeditions he had been a subordinate, but this time he was the leader of 32 colonists.

Champlain and eight others survived the first winter at Quebec and greeted more colonists in June. Allied by an earlier French treaty with the northern Indian tribes, he joined them in defeating Iroquois marauders in a skirmish

EXPLORERS OF THE LATE RENAISSANCE AND THE ENLIGHTENMENT: FROM SIR FRANCIS DRAKE TO MUNGO PARK

Map depicting the explorations of Samuel de Champlain in North America, early 17th century. Encyclopædia Britannica, Inc.

on Lake Champlain. That and a similar victory in 1610 enhanced French prestige among the allied tribes, and fur trade between France and the Indians increased. In 1610 he left for France, where he married Hélène Boullé, the daughter of the secretary to the king's chamber.

The fur trade had heavy financial losses in 1611, which prompted Quebec's sponsors to abandon the colony, but Champlain persuaded Louis XIII to intervene. Eventually the king appointed a viceroy, who made Champlain commandant of New France. In 1613 he reestablished his authority at Quebec and immediately embarked for the Ottawa River on a mission to restore the ruined fur trade. The following year he organized a company of French merchants to finance trade, religious missions, and his own exploration.

Champlain next went to Lake Huron, where native chiefs persuaded him to lead a war party against a fortified village south of Lake Ontario. The Iroquois defenders wounded him and repulsed his Huron-Algonquin warriors, a somewhat disorganized but loyal force, who carried him to safety. After spending a winter in their territory, he returned to France, where political maneuvers were endangering the colony's future. In 1620 the king reaffirmed Champlain's authority over Quebec but forbade his personal exploration, directing him instead to employ his talents in administrative tasks.

The colony, still dependent on the fur trade and only experimenting in agriculture, hardly prospered under his care or under the patronage of a new and strong company. English privateers, however, considered Quebec worth besieging in 1628, when England and France were at war. Champlain manned the walls until the following summer, when his distressed garrison exhausted its food and gunpowder. Although he surrendered the fort, he did

Method used by Indians for hunting deer, illustration from a book by Samuel de Champlain. Library of Congress, Washington, D.C.

not abandon his colony. Taken to England as a prisoner, he argued that the surrender had occurred after the end of French and English hostilities. In 1632 the colony was restored to France, and in 1633, a year after publishing his seventh book, he made his last voyage across the Atlantic Ocean to Quebec.

Only a few more settlers were aboard when his ships dropped anchor at Quebec, but others continued to arrive each year. Before he died of a stroke in 1635, his colony extended along both shores of the St. Lawrence River.

Sir Thomas Button

(d. April 1634)

Sir Thomas Button was an English navigator and naval officer and an early explorer of Canada.

The son of Miles Button of Worleton in Glamorganshire, Wales, Button saw his first naval service in 1588 or 1589, and by 1601, when the Spanish fleet invaded Ireland, he had become captain of the pinnace *Moon*. He acquitted himself with sufficient distinction to win commendation and a lifetime pension of six shillings eight pence. The following year he commanded a privateer, the *Wylloby*, in the West Indies.

In 1612 Button was made a member of the North West Company and given the command of an expedition of two ships—the *Resolution* and the *Discovery*—to North America to try to find and rescue Henry Hudson, whom mutineers had put adrift in a small boat; Button was also to carry on further exploration in hopes of finding the Northwest Passage. The expedition entered Hudson Strait, where he named Resolution Island for his own vessel. The company found no trace of Hudson but made its way through the strait and southwest across Hudson Bay to Nelson River, where it spent a brutal winter. Many men died, including Button's sailing master, for whom the river is named. In the spring and through the summer of 1613 Button and his crew continued their explorations, finally sailing for home in August.

Button was knighted in 1616. He did not return to Canada, although he remained in service. He was a rear admiral in the campaign of 1620–21 against the pirates of the Algerian coast. Button's independent mind and outspoken criticism of the Navy Board, however, led to a reputation for insubordination and a series of legal disputes with the Admiralty. These legal disputes, in addition to his previous debts, impoverished him and remained unresolved at his death.

Dirck Hartog

(fl. 1616)

The Dutch explorer Dirck (or Dirk) Hartog (or Dyrck Hartoochz) made the first recorded exploration of the western coast of Australia.

Traveling an eastward route from Amsterdam around the Cape of Good Hope to Java, Hartog sighted and explored the western Australian coastline. He landed (October 1616) and spent three days exploring a desolate offshore island that he named for himself. To mark his landing, he left a flattened pewter plate, inscribed with the details of the visit, nailed on a post on the northern end of the island, now called Cape Inscription. In 1696 another Dutch explorer, Willem de Vlamingh, landed on Dirk Hartog Island, found Hartog's plate, replaced it with a newly inscribed dish, and sent the original to Amsterdam, where it can now be seen in the Rijksmuseum.

Until the 19th century the coast of Australia parallel to Dirk Hartog Island was called Eendrachtsland, in honour of the explorer's ship, *Eendracht*.

JOHN SMITH

(baptized January 6, 1580, Willoughby, Lincolnshire, England—d. June 21, 1631, London)

The English explorer John Smith was the early leader of the Jamestown Colony, the first permanent English settlement in North America. Smith played an equally important role as a cartographer and a prolific writer who vividly depicted the natural abundance of the New World, whetting the colonizing appetite of prospective English settlers.

Smith grew up on his family's farm in Lincolnshire and was apprenticed in his teens to a wealthy merchant. At age 16 or 17, his adventuresome spirit found an outlet on the battlefields of continental Europe, where he fought for the Netherlands in its war of independence from Spain. Having returned to England by 1599, he spent about two years reading classical military texts and studying horsemanship. He then traveled to Hungary in 1601 as a mercenary to join Austrian forces fighting the Ottoman Empire; he advanced to the rank of captain. Captured by the enemy the following year and taken to Turkey, he escaped to Russia and returned to England in 1604 or 1605.

He then attached himself to a group preparing to establish an English colony in North America. When a royal charter was granted to the Virginia Company of London, Smith and about 100 other colonists led by Christopher Newport set sail on December 20, 1606.

On April 26, 1607, the voyagers arrived at the Chesapeake Bay, and on May 14 they disembarked at what was to become Jamestown. The Virginia Company had named Smith to the colony's seven-member governing council. His relationship with the colony's other leaders was generally antagonistic, his focus being on the practical means of survival in the wilderness rather than on personal privileges and status. He traded for corn (maize) with the local Indians and began a series of river voyages that later enabled him to draw a remarkably accurate map of Virginia. While exploring the Chickahominy River in December 1607, he and his party were ambushed by members of the Powhatan empire, which dominated the region. He was ultimately taken to their ruler, Chief Powhatan, also known as Wahunsenacah. According to Smith's account, he was about to be put to death when he was saved by the chief's young daughter of age 10 or 11, Pocahontas, who placed herself between him and his executioners.

Smith became president of the Jamestown Colony on September 10, 1608. He conducted military training and continued to secure corn from the Indians by trade. He required greater discipline of the colonists, announcing a policy that "he that will not worke shall not eate (except by sicknesse he be disabled)." Colonists had previously been fed from a common storehouse whether they worked or not. Under Smith's direction, small quantities of tar, pitch, and soap ash were made, a well was dug, houses were built, fishing was done regularly, crops were planted, and outlying forts were built. The colony

Pocahontas saving John Smith from execution. © SuperStock

bore little loss of life during his presidency, compared with the enormous suffering and mortality of the years before and after his rule. In his dealings with Native Americans, Smith's approach differed from those of the Spanish conquistadores and later English settlers. Smith chose to keep the Powhatan empire at bay through psychology, diplomacy, and intimidation—not massacre. He believed the English could avoid bloodshed by projecting an image of strength. When Smith was injured from a fire in his powder bag in September 1609, he was forced to return to England.

Still eager to explore and settle in America, Smith made contact with the Plymouth Company and sailed in

EXPLORERS OF THE LATE RENAISSANCE AND THE ENLIGHTENMENT: FROM SIR FRANCIS DRAKE TO MUNGO PARK

1614 to the area he named New England, carefully mapping the coast from Penobscot Bay to Cape Cod. On another exploratory voyage the following year, he was captured by pirates and returned to England after escaping three months later. In 1617 he made one final colonizing attempt, but his vessels were unable to leave port for three months for lack of winds, and he never set sail.

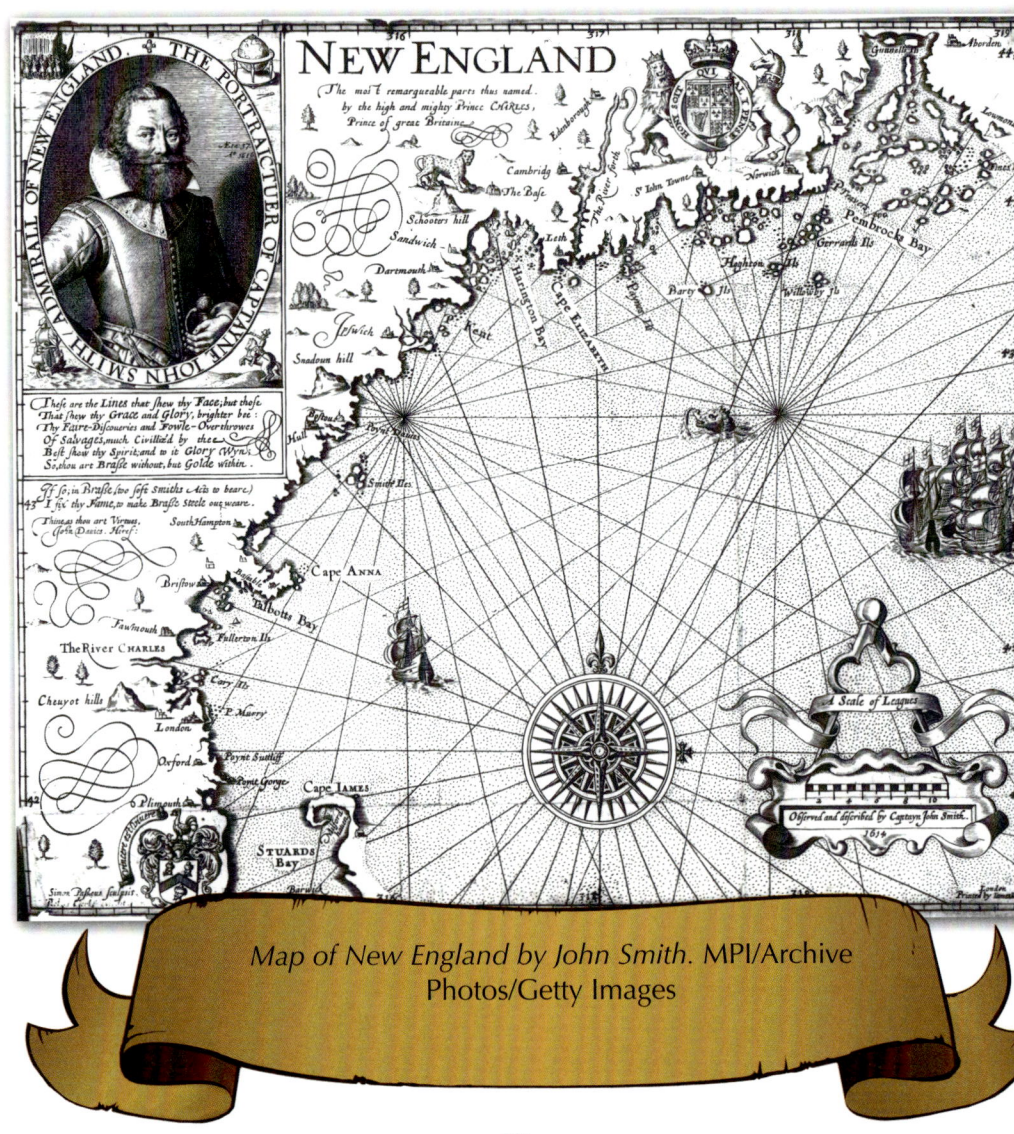

Map of New England by John Smith. MPI/Archive Photos/Getty Images

Smith advocated English settlement of New England for the rest of his life, but he never saw North America again. His writings include detailed descriptions of Virginia and New England, books on seamanship, and a history of English colonization. Among his books are *A Description of New England* (1616), a counterpart to his *Map of Virginia with a Description of the Country* (1612); *The Generall Historie of Virginia, New England, and the Summer Isles* (1624); and *The True Travels, Adventures, and Observations of Captain John Smith in Europe, Asia, Africa, and America* (1630). The *Mayflower* colonists of 1620 brought his books and maps with them to Massachusetts. Smith died of an unrecorded illness midway through 1631, at age 51, in the London home of Sir Samuel Saltonstall, a friend.

During the founding years of the United States in the late 18th and the early 19th century, Smith was widely regarded as a reliable observer as well as a national hero. Thomas Jefferson described him as "honest, sensible, and well informed." Some historians have contended that Smith was prone to self-promotion in his writings. Yet his writings are notably generous in giving credit to others who helped the colony survive, and scholars have confirmed factual details of his autobiographical writing.

Smith's account of his rescue by Pocahontas in 1607 has been particularly controversial. Some scholars believe he might have misunderstood the event—that it could have been an adoption ceremony rather than an intended execution—and others contend that he fabricated the incident outright. With regard to the truthfulness of Smith's account, it has been argued that he had little reason to concoct such an episode. Because Smith was the only English eyewitness to the incident and the Powhatan witnesses left no written record, the debate over it may never be conclusively resolved.

William Baffin

(b. c. 1584, London, England?—d. January 23, 1622, Persian Gulf, off the island of Qeshm [now part of Iran])

The English navigator and explorer William Baffin searched for the Northwest Passage and gave his name to Baffin Island, now part of the territory of Nunavut, Canada, and to the bay separating it from Greenland. His determination of longitude at sea by observing the occultation of a star by the Moon in 1615 is said to have been the first of its kind on record.

The earliest mention of Baffin (1612) was as a member of Captain James Hall's expedition in search of the Northwest Passage. Aboard the *Discovery* with Captain Robert Bylot (1615), Baffin explored Hudson Strait, which separates Canada from Baffin Island. In 1616 Baffin again sailed as pilot of the *Discovery* and penetrated Baffin Bay some 300 miles (483 km) farther than the English navigator John Davis had in 1587. In honour of the patrons of his voyages, he named Lancaster, Smith, and Jones sounds, the straits radiating from the northern head of the bay. There seemed to be no hope, however, of discovering a passage to India by that route.

Next, in service to the East India Company, he made surveys of the Red Sea and the Persian Gulf. In 1622, during his final voyage to the Persian Gulf, he was killed in an Anglo-Persian attack on Qeshm.

Anthony van Diemen

(b. 1593, Culemborg, Netherlands—d. April 19, 1645, Batavia, Dutch East Indies [now Indonesia])

Anthony van Diemen was a colonial administrator who as governor-general of the Dutch East Indian settlements (1636–45) consolidated the Dutch interests in Southeast Asia.

After an unsuccessful business career in Amsterdam, van Diemen joined the Dutch East India Company, serving in Batavia (now Jakarta, Indonesia) from 1618 and becoming governor-general in 1636. To strengthen the company's rule in the Moluccas, he signed a treaty with the sultan of Ternate in 1638, which freed the company for a war of conquest (1638–43) and resulted in a Dutch spice monopoly in the area. Also in 1638 van Diemen intensified the Dutch attack on Portuguese holdings in Asia with an invasion of Ceylon (Sri Lanka). By 1644 the Dutch had conquered Ceylon's cinnamon-producing areas and had established posts on India's Coromandel Coast.

Meanwhile, van Diemen had succeeded in seizing the key Portuguese stronghold of Malacca (1641; Melaka, now in Malaysia) on the trade route between India and China, and in 1642 the Dutch captured all of Formosa (Taiwan), driving out the Spanish. Under his rule, advantageous treaties with the East Indian princes of Aceh (Acheh; Atjeh) and Tidore were signed, and commercial relations with

Tonkin (Vietnam) and Japan were established. By the end of van Diemen's administration, the United Provinces of the Netherlands had become the paramount commercial and political power in insular Southeast Asia.

Van Diemen completed the construction of Batavia in the Dutch pattern of his predecessor, Jan Pieterszoon Coen, including a Latin school, Protestant churches, an orphanage, and a hospital; he also introduced a legal code known as the Batavian statutes. Van Diemen initiated the exploring expeditions of Abel Janszoon Tasman and Frans Visscher in 1642 and 1644 on which they discovered Tasmania (originally called Van Diemen's Land), New Zealand, Tonga, Fiji, and the northern coast of Australia.

Jean Nicolet

(b. 1598, Cherbourg, France—d. November 1, 1642, Sillery, Quebec, Canada)

The French North American explorer Jean Nicolet was the first known European to discover Lake Michigan and what is now the state of Wisconsin.

The son of a dispatch carrier, Nicolet was 20 years old when he traveled to New France (Canada) at the request of Samuel de Champlain. He lived with a friendly Indian tribe on Allumette Island in the Ottawa River, learned the Algonquian language and culture, and participated in negotiations with the Iroquois. He returned to Quebec in 1620 and was then sent to live among the distant

Nipissing tribe. In 1624 he became their interpreter. Nine years later he returned to the Three Rivers settlement in New France and became the colony's official interpreter.

In early 1634 Nicolet joined an expedition that journeyed westward into the Huron territory. There he obtained a large canoe and with seven Huron braves proceeded from Lake Huron through the Straits of Mackinac to discover Lake Michigan. The lake was not the Northwest Passage to the Pacific Ocean that Nicolet anticipated, but he paddled southward to Green Bay and there concluded a friendship treaty with the Winnebago tribe.

Nicolet explored the region of present-day Wisconsin for a short time before he returned to Quebec during the autumn of 1634. He resumed his duties as colony interpreter and earned considerable respect from both French settlers and local Indian tribes. Nicolet was drowned when his boat capsized during a sudden storm on the St. Lawrence River.

ABEL JANSZOON TASMAN

(b. 1603?, Lutjegast, Netherlands—
d. probably before October 22, 1659,
certainly before February 5, 1661)

Abel Janszoon Tasman, who discovered Tasmania, New Zealand, Tonga, and the Fiji Islands, was the greatest of the Dutch navigators and explorers. On his first voyage (1642–43) in the service of the Dutch East India Company,

Abel Tasman with his family. Popperfoto/Getty Image

Tasman explored the Indian Ocean, Australasia, and the southern Pacific Ocean; on his second voyage (1644) he traveled in Australian and South Pacific waters.

Tasman entered the service of the Dutch East India Company in 1632 or 1633 and made his first voyage of exploration to Ceram (modern Seram) Island (in modern Indonesia) as captain of the *Mocha* in 1634. He sailed in 1639 under Commander Mathijs Hendrickszoon Quast on an expedition in search of the "islands of gold and silver" in the seas east of Japan. After a series of trading voyages to Japan, Formosa (Taiwan), Cambodia, and Sumatra, he was chosen by the governor-general of the Dutch East Indies, Anthony van Diemen, to command the most ambitious of all Dutch voyages for the exploration of the Southern Hemisphere.

By 1642, Dutch navigators had discovered discontinuous stretches of the western coast of Australia, but whether these coasts were continental and connected with the hypothetical southern continent of the Pacific remained unknown. Tasman was assigned to solve this problem, following instructions based on a memoir by Frans Jacobszoon Visscher, his chief pilot. He was instructed to explore the Indian Ocean from west to east, south of the ordinary trade route, and, proceeding eastward into the Pacific (if this proved possible), to investigate the practicability of a sea passage eastward to Chile, to rediscover the Solomon Islands of the Spaniards, and to explore New Guinea.

Leaving Batavia (modern Jakarta) on August 14, 1642, with two ships, the *Heemskerk* and *Zeehaen*, Tasman sailed to Mauritius (September 5–October 8), then southward and eastward, reaching his most southerly latitude of 49° S at about longitude 94° E. Turning north he discovered land on November 24 at 42°20´ S, and he skirted its southern shores, naming it Van Diemen's Land (now Tasmania). A council of officers on December 5 decided against further investigation, so he missed the opportunity to discover Bass Strait. Continuing eastward, he sighted on December 13, at 42°10´ S, the coast of South Island, New Zealand, and explored it northward, entering the strait between North Island and South Island, supposing it to be a bay. He left New Zealand on January 4, 1643, at North Cape, under the impression that he had probably discovered the west coast of the southern continent, which might be connected with the "Staten Landt" (Staten Island) discovered by W.C. Schouten and Jacques Le Maire south of South America—hence the name of Staten Landt, which Tasman gave to his discovery in honour of the States General (the Dutch legislature).

Convinced by the swell that the passage to Chile existed, Tasman now turned northeast, and on January 21 he discovered Tonga and on February 6 the Fiji Islands. Turning northwest, the ships reached New Guinea waters on April 1 and Batavia on June 14, 1643, completing a 10-month voyage on which only 10 men had died from illness. Tasman had circumnavigated Australia without seeing it, thus establishing that it was separated from the hypothetical southern continent.

The council of the company decided, however, that Tasman had been negligent in his investigation of the lands that he discovered and of the passage to Chile. They sent him on a new expedition to the "South Land" in 1644 with instructions to establish the relationships of New Guinea, the "great known South Land" (western Australia), Van Diemen's Land, and the "unknown South Land." Tasman sailed from Batavia on February 29, steering southeast along the south coast of New Guinea, sailing southeast into Torres Strait (which he mistook for a shallow bay), coasting Australia's Gulf of Carpentaria, and then following the north coast and then the west coast of Australia to 22° S.

Although he was rewarded with the rank of commander and was made a member of the Council of Justice of Batavia, his second voyage was also a disappointment to the company because it had failed to reveal lands of potential wealth. In 1647 Tasman commanded a trading fleet to Siam (now Thailand), and in the following year he commanded a war fleet against the Spaniards in the Philippines. He left the service of the Dutch East India Company several years later.

Semyon Ivanov Dezhnyov

(b. c. 1605, Veliky Ustyug, Russia—d. early 1673, Moscow)

The Russian explorer Semyon Ivanov Dezhnyov (or Dezhnëv) was the first European known to have sailed through the Bering Strait separating northeastern Asia and northwestern North America.

Dezhnyov served as a Cossack soldier in Siberia, where he traveled a great deal in the north beginning in the early 1640s. In 1648 he sailed from the Kolyma River eastward to the Bering Strait, rounding the northeast tip of Asia (now called Cape Dezhnyov) and reaching the Anadyr River. He thus proved the separation of Asia and North America, but his report lay buried in the archives at Yakutsk until the German historian Gerhard Friedrich Müller found it in 1736; thus the discovery was not known about until nearly a century had passed and after the Danish navigator Vitus Bering and others had explored the area.

Louis Hennepin

(b. May 12, 1626, Ath, Belgium—d. after 1701, Rome?)

Louis Hennepin was a Franciscan missionary who, with the celebrated French explorer René-Robert Cavelier, sieur de La Salle, penetrated the Great Lakes in 1679 to the region of Illinois and wrote the first published description of the country.

Hennepin joined the Récollet Order of Friars Minor, Béthune, France, and in 1675 went to Canada with La Salle, whose chaplain he became in 1678. Together they reached the site of Peoria, Illinois (January 1680), where they established Fort Crèvecoeur. La Salle then returned to Fort Frontenac (at Kingston, Ontario) for supplies, while Hennepin and the remainder of the party explored the upper Mississippi River. In April they were captured by Sioux Indians, whom they accompanied on several hunting expeditions, during the course of which they reached what Hennepin named the Falls of St. Anthony (site of Minneapolis, Minnesota). Hennepin was rescued by the French voyageur Daniel Greysolon, sieur DuLhut, in July 1680. Returning to France in 1682, he wrote a full account of his exploits, *Description de la Louisiane* (1683), later revised as *Nouvelle découverte d'un très grand pays situé dans l'Amérique* (1697; "New Discovery of a Very Large Country Situated in America"), in which he claimed to have explored the Mississippi to its mouth. This bold assumption was, however, soon discredited. Hennepin spent his final years in obscurity, being last heard of in a Roman monastery in 1701.

JACQUES MARQUETTE

(b. June 1, 1637, Laon, France—d. May 18, 1675, Ludington [now in Michigan, U.S.])

Jacques Marquette—also known as Père (Father) Marquette—was a French Jesuit missionary explorer

JACQUES MARQUETTE

who, with Louis Jolliet, traveled down the Mississippi River and reported the first accurate data on its course.

Marquette arrived in Quebec in 1666. After a study of Indian languages, he assisted in founding a mission at Sault Ste. Marie (now in Michigan) in 1668, and another at St. Ignace (also now in Michigan) in 1671. In mid-May 1673 he left St. Ignace with Jolliet, who had been commissioned by Louis, comte de Frontenac, governor of New France, to find the direction and the mouth of the Mississippi. They traveled westward to Green Bay (now in Wisconsin), ascended the Fox River to a portage that crossed to the Wisconsin River, and entered the Mississippi near present-day Prairie du Chien on June 17. Following it to the mouth

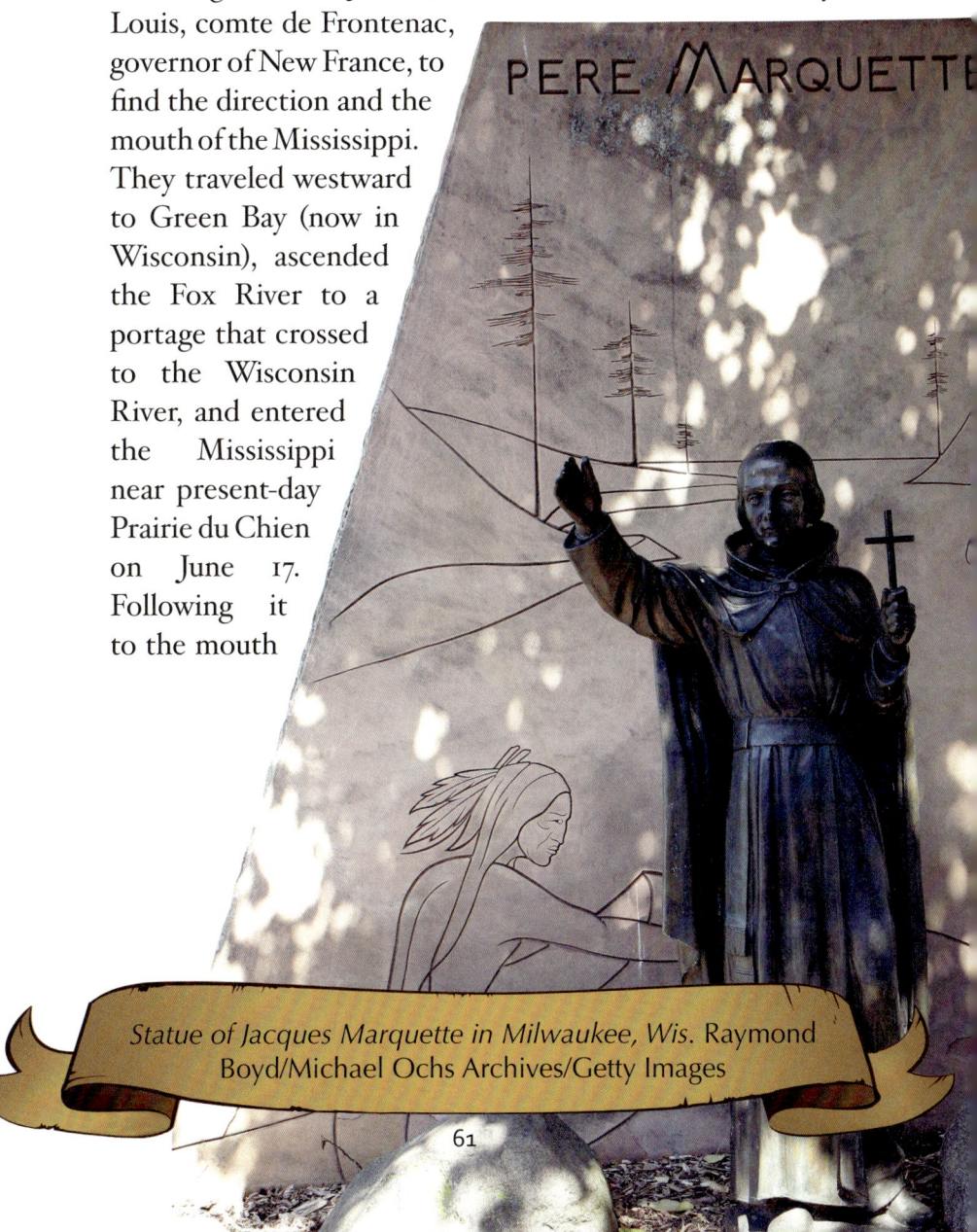

Statue of Jacques Marquette in Milwaukee, Wis. Raymond Boyd/Michael Ochs Archives/Getty Images

of the Arkansas River, they learned that the Mississippi flowed through hostile Spanish domains, and in mid-July they turned homeward by way of the Illinois River. Marquette was exhausted when he reached Green Bay, and he remained there while Jolliet continued on to Canada.

In 1674 Marquette set out to found a mission among the Illinois Indians, but, caught by the winter, he and two companions camped near the site of the modern city of Chicago, and thus became the first Europeans to live there. Marquette reached the Indians (near what is now Utica, Illinois) in the spring, but illness forced his return. While en route to St. Ignace he died at the mouth of a stream now known as Père Marquette River.

Daniel Greysolon, sieur DuLhut

(b. c. 1639, Saint-Germain-Laval, near Lyon, France—d. February 25/26, 1710, Montreal [now in Quebec, Canada])

The French soldier and explorer Daniel Greysolon, sieur DuLhut—whose title is also spelled Du Lhut, Du Luth, or Duluth—was largely responsible for establishing French control over the country north and west of Lake Superior. The city of Duluth, Minnesota, was named for him.

DuLhut became an ensign in the regiment at Lyon in 1657, and about 1665 he became an officer in the royal household regiment. He fought against the Dutch under the Great Condé in 1674, by which time he had already made two voyages to New France.

In 1675 he returned to Montreal until September 1678, when he led a party of Frenchmen and three Indian slaves to the Lake Superior country, where he hoped to negotiate peace among the Indian tribes north and west of the lake (a rich source of beaver pelts). In September 1679 DuLhut was able to bring the Indians together in a seemingly successful assembly in which amity was declared among the tribes. After wintering in the West, DuLhut decided to move farther west the next summer in search of the western ocean. The party penetrated well into what is now Minnesota and reached the Mississippi River.

On returning to Montreal, DuLhut found himself accused as a renegade trader, in violation of a 1676 edict prohibiting Frenchmen from venturing into the woods as traders. He returned to France to clear his name but was back in 1682 and the next year went off again to the West to renew his peacemaking efforts and to try to dissuade the Indians from trading their pelts to the English. He also raised Indian support for French troops and campaigned with Louis de Frontenac against the Indian allies of the British, the Oneida and Onondaga. In 1696 he was in command at Fort Frontenac. Thereafter he retired to spend his remaining years in Montreal.

Pierre-Esprit Radisson

(b. c. 1640, Avignon?, France—d. c. 1710, England?)

Pierre-Esprit Radisson was a French explorer and fur trader who served both France and England in Canada. He arrived in New France possibly in 1651 and settled at Trois-Rivières. In that year he was captured and adopted by Iroquois Indians, with whom he chose to remain despite opportunities to escape. Later he left North America and sailed to France, landing at La Rochelle early in 1654.

Radisson returned to Canada the same year. With his brother-in-law, Médard Chouart des Groseilliers, he spent the next few years on trading expeditions to the West. In 1658 they set out for Lake Nipissing (then known as Lac des Castors), crossing what is now Wisconsin and the upper Mississippi River Valley. Because they had failed to secure a government license, the French authorities in 1663 confiscated their furs and fined them. As a result Radisson and Groseilliers offered their services to the English at Port-Royal (now Annapolis Royal, Nova Scotia).

They were later employed by New Englanders of Boston, for whom they sailed to Hudson Strait and discovered copper deposits near Lake Superior. Their report on the wealth in furs led to the formation of the Hudson's Bay Company in 1670. Financed by Prince Rupert, cousin to King Charles II, Radisson undertook another trading expedition in 1668 in search of a Northwest Passage. In

1671 he founded Moose Factory, a company trading post a few miles south of James Bay.

Three years later, Radisson and Groseilliers made their peace with France and served in the French fleet in Guinea and Tobago. Radisson became a resident of Quebec in 1681, and the following year he led an expedition against the English on Hudson Bay. After revisiting both France and England, he was again employed by the Hudson's Bay Company and was eventually pensioned by the company.

René-Robert Cavelier, sieur de La Salle

(b. November 22, 1643, Rouen, France—d. March 19, 1687, near the Brazos River [now in Texas, U.S.])

The French colonist and renowned explorer of North America René-Robert Cavelier, sieur de La Salle, led an expedition down the Illinois and Mississippi rivers and claimed all the region watered by the Mississippi and its tributaries for Louis XIV of France, naming the region "Louisiana." A few years later, in another and ultimately luckless expedition seeking the mouth of the Mississippi, he was murdered by his men.

EARLY LIFE

La Salle was educated at a Jesuit college. He first studied for the priesthood, but at the age of 22 he found himself

René-Robert Cavelier, sieur de La Salle. Encyclopædia Britannica, Inc.

more attracted to adventure and exploration and in 1666 set out for Canada to seek his fortune. With a grant of land at the western end of Île de Montréal, La Salle acquired at one stroke the status of a seigneur (i.e., landholder) and the opportunities of a frontiersman.

The young landlord farmed his land near the Lachine Rapids and, at the same time, set up a fur-trading outpost. Through contact with the Indians who came to sell their pelts, he learned various Indian dialects and heard stories of the lands beyond the settlements. He soon became obsessed with the idea of finding a way to Asia through the rivers and lakes of the Western frontier.

If experience modified the visions of the dreamer, it enhanced the knowledge and skill of the pathfinder and trader. Having sold his land, La Salle set out in 1669 to explore the Ohio region. His discovery of the Ohio River, however, is not accepted by modern historians.

La Salle found a kindred spirit in the Count de Frontenac, the "Fighting Governor" of New France (the French possessions in Canada) from 1672 to 1682. Together, they pursued a policy of extending French military power by establishing a fort on Lake Ontario (Fort Frontenac), holding the Iroquois in check, and intercepting the fur trade between the Upper Lakes and the Dutch and English coastal settlements.

Their plans were strongly opposed by the Montreal merchants, who feared the loss of their trade, and by the missionaries (especially the Jesuits), who were afraid of losing their influence over the Indians of the interior. Nevertheless, Fort Frontenac was built where Kingston, Ontario, now stands, and La Salle was installed there as seigneur in 1675 after a visit to the French court, as Frontenac's representative. The governor had recommended him as "a man of intelligence and ability, more capable than anybody else I know here to accomplish every kind of enterprise and discovery." Louis XIV was sufficiently impressed by him to grant him a title of nobility.

ATTEMPTS TO EXPAND NEW FRANCE

At Fort Frontenac, La Salle had control of a large share of the fur trade, and his affairs prospered. But his restless ambition drove him to seek greater ends. On another visit to France in 1677 he obtained from the king authority to explore "the western parts of New France" and permission to build as many forts as he wished, as well as to hold a valuable monopoly of the trade in buffalo hides.

Since the project had to be carried out at his own expense, however, he borrowed large sums in both Paris and Montreal, and he began to be enmeshed in a tangle of debts that was to blight all of his later enterprises. La Salle's proposals also roused still further the enmity of the Jesuits, who resolutely opposed all his schemes.

When he returned to Canada in 1678, La Salle was accompanied by an Italian soldier of fortune, Henri de Tonty, who became his most loyal friend and ally. Early in the following year, he built the *Griffon*, the first commercial sailing vessel on Lake Erie, which he hoped would pay for an expedition into the interior as far as the Mississippi. From the Seneca Indians above the Niagara Falls he learned how to make long journeys overland, on foot in any season, subsisting on game and a small bag of corn (maize). His trek from Niagara to Fort Frontenac in the dead of winter won the admiration of a normally critical member of his expeditions, the friar Louis Hennepin.

La Salle's great scheme of carrying cargo in sailing vessels like the *Griffon* on the lakes and down the Mississippi was frustrated by the wreck of that ship and by the destruction and desertion of Fort Crèvecoeur (present-day Peoria, Illinois) on the Illinois River, which he and Tonty had constructed and where a second ship was being built in 1680. Proud and unyielding by nature, La Salle tried to bend others to his will and often demanded too much of them, though he was no less hard on himself. After several disappointments, he at last reached the junction of the Illinois with the Mississippi and saw for the first time the river he had dreamed of for so long. But he had to deny himself the chance to explore it. Hearing that Tonty and his party were in danger, he turned back to aid them.

After many vicissitudes, La Salle and Tonty succeeded in canoeing down the Mississippi and reached the Gulf of Mexico. There, on April 9, 1682, the explorer proclaimed the whole Mississippi Basin for France and named it Louisiana. In name, at least, he acquired for France the most fertile portion of the North American continent.

The following year La Salle built Fort St. Louis at Starved Rock on the Illinois River (now an Illinois state park), and here he organized a colony of several thousand Indians. To maintain the new colony he sought help from Quebec; but Frontenac had been replaced by a governor hostile to La Salle's interests, and La Salle received orders to surrender Fort St. Louis. He refused and left North America to appeal directly to the king. Welcomed in Paris, La Salle was given an audience with Louis XIV, who favoured him by commanding the governor to make full restitution of La Salle's property.

LAST EXPEDITION

The last phase of his extraordinary career centred on his proposal to fortify the mouth of the Mississippi and to invade and conquer part of the Spanish province of Mexico. He planned to accomplish all this with some 200 Frenchmen, aided by buccaneers and an army of 15,000 Indians—a venture that caused his detractors to question his sanity. But the king saw a chance to harass the Spaniards, with whom he was at war, and approved the project, giving La Salle men, ships, and money.

The expedition was doomed from the start. It had hardly left France when quarrels arose between La Salle and the naval commander. Vessels were lost by piracy and shipwreck, while sickness took a heavy toll of the colonists. Finally, a gross miscalculation brought the ships to Matagorda Bay in Texas, 500 miles (800 km) west of their intended landfall. After several fruitless journeys in search of his lost Mississippi, La Salle met his death at the hands of mutineers near the Brazos River. His vision of a French empire died with him.

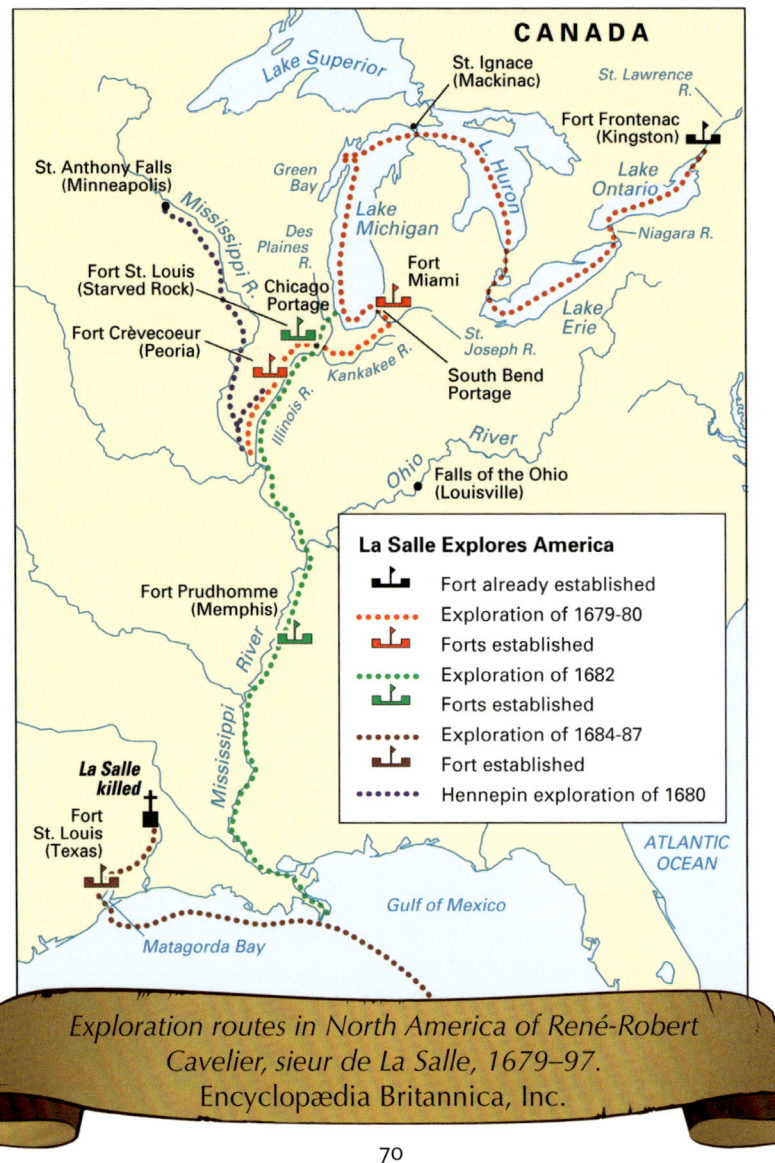

Exploration routes in North America of René-Robert Cavelier, sieur de La Salle, 1679–97. Encyclopædia Britannica, Inc.

La Salle provoked much controversy both in his own lifetime and later. Those who knew him best praised his ability unsparingly. He was considered "one of the greatest men of the age" by Tonty, who, like Frontenac, was among the very few who were able to understand the proud spirit of the dour Norman. Henri Joutel, who served under La Salle through the tragic days of the Texas colony until his death, wrote both of his fine qualities and of his insufferable arrogance toward his subordinates. In Joutel's view, this arrogance was the true cause of La Salle's death.

Undoubtedly, La Salle was hampered by faults of character and lacked the qualities of leadership. On the other hand, he possessed prodigious vision, tenacity, and courage. His claim of Louisiana for France, though but a vain boast at the time, pointed the way to the French colonial empire that was eventually built by other men.

William Penn

(b. October 14, 1644, London, England—d. July 30, 1718, Buckinghamshire)

The English Quaker leader and advocate of religious freedom William Penn oversaw the founding of the American Commonwealth of Pennsylvania as a refuge for Quakers and other religious minorities of Europe.

Explorers of the Late Renaissance and the Enlightenment: From Sir Francis Drake to Mungo Park

William Penn. Stock Montage/Archive Photos/Getty Images

EARLY LIFE AND EDUCATION

William was the son of Admiral Sir William Penn. He acquired the foundations of a classical education at the Chigwell grammar school in the Essex countryside, where he came under Puritan influences. After Admiral Penn's naval defeat in the West Indies in 1655, the family moved back to London and then to Ireland. In Ireland William heard Thomas Loe, a Quaker itinerant, preach to his family at the admiral's invitation, an experience that apparently intensified his religious feelings. In 1660 William entered the University of Oxford, where he rejected Anglicanism and was expelled in 1662 for his religious nonconformity. Determined to thwart his son's religiosity, Admiral Penn sent young William on a grand tour of the European continent and to the Protestant college at Saumur, in France, to complete his studies. Summoned back to England after two years, William entered Lincoln's Inn and spent a year reading law. This was the extent of his formal education.

In 1666 Admiral Penn sent William to Ireland to manage the family estates. There he crossed paths again with Thomas Loe and, after hearing him preach, decided to join the Quakers (the Society of Friends), a sect of religious radicals who were reviled by respectable society and subject to official persecution.

QUAKER LEADERSHIP AND POLITICAL ACTIVISM

After joining the sect, Penn would eventually be imprisoned four times for publicly stating his beliefs in word and print. He published 42 books and pamphlets in the seven years immediately following his conversion. In his first publication, the pamphlet *Truth Exalted* (1668), he upheld Quaker doctrines while attacking in turn those of the Roman Catholics, the Anglicans, and the Dissenting churches. It was followed by *The Sandy Foundation Shaken* (1668), in which he boldly questioned the Trinity and other Protestant doctrines. Though Penn subsequently qualified his anti-Trinitarianism in *Innocency with Her Open Face* (1669), he was imprisoned in the Tower of London, where he wrote his most famous book, *No Cross, No Crown* (1669). In this work he expounded the Quaker-Puritan morality with eloquence, learning, and flashes of humour, condemning the worldliness and luxury of Restoration England and extolling both Puritan conceptions of ascetic self-denial and Quaker ideals of social reform. *No Cross, No Crown* stands alongside the letters of St. Paul, Boethius's *Consolation of Philosophy*, and John Bunyan's *Pilgrim's Progress* as one of the world's finest examples of prison literature. Penn was released from the Tower in 1669.

It was as a protagonist of religious toleration that Penn would earn his prominent place in English history. In 1670 he wrote *The Great Case of Liberty of Conscience Once More Debated & Defended*, which was the most systematic and thorough exposition of the theory of toleration produced in Restoration England. Though Penn based his arguments on theological and scriptural grounds, he did not overlook rational and pragmatic considerations; he pointed out, for example, that the contemporary prosperity of Holland was based on "her Indulgence in matters of Faith and Worship."

That same year Penn also had an unexpected opportunity to strike another blow for freedom of conscience and for the traditional rights of all Englishmen. On August 14, 1670, the Quaker meetinghouse in Gracechurch Street, London, having been padlocked by the authorities, he preached in the street to several hundred persons. After the meetings, he and William Mead were arrested and imprisoned on a trumped-up charge of inciting a riot. At his trial in the Old Bailey, Penn calmly and skillfully exposed the illegality of the proceedings against him. The jury, under the leadership of Edward Bushell, refused to bring in a verdict of guilty despite threats and abusive treatment. For their refusal the jurymen were fined and imprisoned, but they were vindicated when Sir John Vaughan, the lord chief justice, enunciated the principle that a judge "may try to open the eyes of the jurors, but not to lead them by the nose." The trial, which is also known as the "Bushell's Case," stands as a landmark in English legal history, having established beyond question the independence of the jury. A firsthand account of the trial, which was a vivid courtroom drama, was published in *The People's Ancient and Just Liberties Asserted* (1670).

Admiral Penn died in 1670, having finally become reconciled to his son's Quakerism. Young Penn inherited his father's estates in England and Ireland and became, like his father, a frequenter of the court, where he enjoyed the friendship of King Charles II and his brother, the duke of York (later James II). In 1672 Penn married Gulielma Springett, a Quaker by whom he had eight children, four of whom died in infancy. In the 1670s Penn was tirelessly active as a Quaker minister and polemicist, producing no fewer than 40 controversial tracts on religious doctrines and practice. In 1671 and 1677 he undertook preaching missions to Holland and northern Germany, where the contacts he established would later help him in peopling Pennsylvania with thousands of Dutch and German emigrants. The later years of the decade were also occupied with political activities. In 1679 Penn supported the Parliamentary candidacy of the radical republican Algernon Sidney, going on the hustings twice—at

Guildford and later at Bramber—for his friend. During these years he wrote a number of pamphlets on behalf of the radical Whigs, including *England's Great Interest in the Choice of this New Parliament* (1679), which is noteworthy as one of the first clear statements of party doctrine ever laid before the English electorate.

FOUNDING AND GOVERNORSHIP OF PENNSYLVANIA

Penn had meanwhile become involved in American colonization as a trustee for Edward Byllynge, one of the two Quaker proprietors of West New Jersey. In 1681 Penn and 11 other Quakers bought the proprietary rights to East New Jersey from the widow of Sir John Carteret. In that same year, discouraged by the turn of political events in England, where Charles II was ruling without Parliament and prospects for religious freedom seemed dark, Penn sought and received a vast province on the west bank of the Delaware River, which was named Pennsylvania after his father (to whom Charles II had owed a large debt canceled by this grant). A few months later the duke of York granted him the three "lower counties" (later Delaware). In Pennsylvania Penn hoped to provide a refuge for Quakers and other persecuted people and to build an ideal Christian commonwealth. "There may be room there, though not here" he wrote to a friend in America, "for such a holy experiment."

As proprietor, Penn seized the opportunity to create a government that would embody his Quaker-Whig ideas. In 1682 he drew up a Frame of Government for

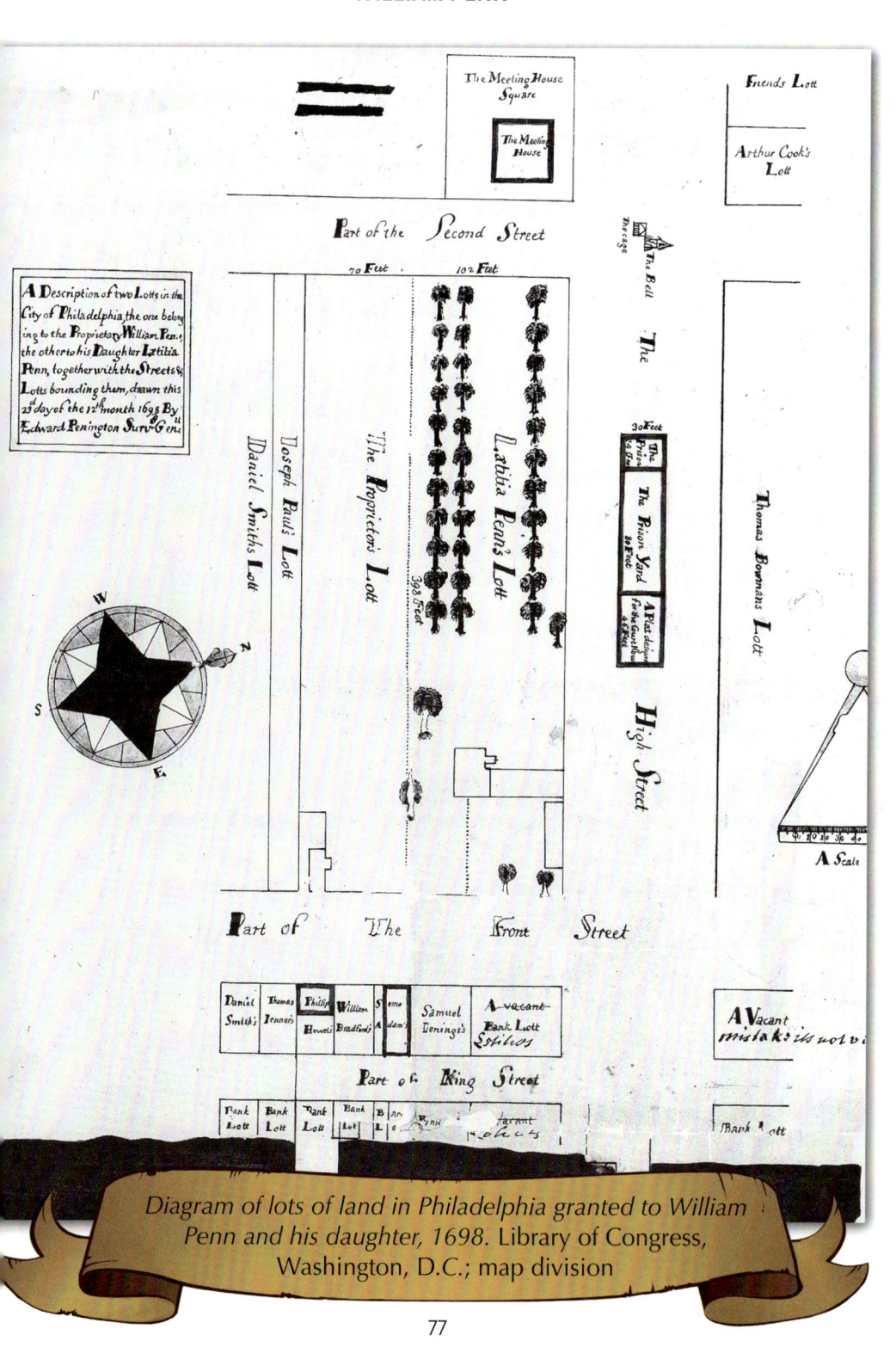

Diagram of lots of land in Philadelphia granted to William Penn and his daughter, 1698. Library of Congress, Washington, D.C.; map division

the colony that would, he said, leave himself and his successors "no power of doing mischief, that the will of one man may not hinder the good of a whole country." Freedom of worship in the colony was to be absolute, and all the traditional rights of Englishmen were carefully safeguarded. The actual machinery of government outlined in the Frame proved in some respects to be clumsy and unworkable, but Penn wisely included in the Frame an amending clause—the first in any written constitution—so that it could be altered as necessity required.

Penn himself sailed in the *Welcome* for Pennsylvania late in 1682, leaving his family behind, and found his experiment already well under way. The city of Philadelphia was already laid out on a grid pattern according to his instructions, and settlers were pouring in to take up the fertile lands lying around it. Presiding over the first Assembly, Penn saw the government of the "lower counties" united with that of Pennsylvania and the Frame of Government incorporated in the Great Law of the province. In a series of treaties based on mutual trust, he established good relations with the Lenni Lenape Indians. He also held an unsuccessful conference with Lord Baltimore, the proprietor of the neighbouring province of Maryland, to negotiate a boundary between it and Pennsylvania. When this effort proved unsuccessful, Penn was obliged in 1684 to return to England to defend his interests against Baltimore.

Before his return, he published *A Letter to the Free Society of Traders* (1683), which contained his fullest description of Pennsylvania and included a valuable account of the Lenni Lenape (Delaware Indians) based on firsthand observation. With the accession of his friend the duke of York as James II in 1685, Penn found himself in a position of great influence at court, whereby he was able to have hundreds of Quakers, as well as political prisoners such as John Locke, released from prison. Penn welcomed James's Declaration of Indulgence (1687) but received some criticism for doing so, since the declaration provided religious toleration at the royal pleasure rather than as a matter of fundamental right. But the Act of Toleration (1689), passed after James's abdication, finally established the principle for which Penn had laboured so long and faithfully.

Penn's close relations with James brought him under a cloud when William and Mary came to the throne, and for a time he was forced to live virtually in hiding to avoid arrest. He used this period of forced retirement to write more books. Among them were *An Essay Towards the Present and Future Peace of Europe* (1693), in which he proposed an international organization to prevent wars by arbitrating disputes, and *A Brief Account of the Rise and Progress of the People Called Quakers* (1694), which was the earliest serious effort to set down the history of the Quaker movement. Penn also drafted (1696) the first plan for a future union of the American colonies, a document that presaged the U.S. Constitution.

In 1696, his first wife having died in 1694, Penn married Hannah Callowhill, by whom he had seven children, five of whom lived to adulthood. Meanwhile, affairs had been going badly in Pennsylvania. For about two years (1692–94), while Penn was under suspicion, the government of the colony had been taken from him and given to that of New York. Afterwards, Pennsylvania's Assembly quarreled constantly with its Council and with Penn's deputy governors. The "lower counties" were unhappy at being unequally yoked with the larger province of Pennsylvania. Relations with the home government were strained by the Quakers' conscientious refusal to provide military defense. In 1699 Penn, his wife, and his secretary, James Logan, returned to the province. He settled many of the outstanding difficulties, though he was compelled to grant the Pennsylvania Assembly preeminence in 1701 in a revised constitution known as the Charter of Privileges. He also allowed the lower counties to form their own independent government. After less than two years Penn's affairs in England demanded his presence, and he left the province in 1701, never to see it again. He confided his Pennsylvania interests to the capable hands of James Logan, who upheld them loyally for the next half century.

FINAL YEARS

Penn's final years were unhappy. His eldest son, William, Jr., turned out a scapegrace. Penn's own poor judgment in choosing his subordinates (except for the faithful Logan) recoiled upon him: his deputy governors proved incompetent or untrustworthy, and his steward, Philip Ford, cheated him on such a staggering scale that Penn was forced to spend nine months in a debtors' prison. In 1712, discouraged at the outcome of his "holy experiment," Penn began negotiations to surrender Pennsylvania to the English crown. A paralytic stroke, which seriously impaired his memory and dulled his once-keen intellect, prevented the consummation of these negotiations. Penn lingered on, virtually helpless, until 1718, his wife undertaking to manage his proprietary affairs. Penn's collected works were published in 1726.

Louis Jolliet

(b. before September 21, 1645, probably Beaupré, near Quebec— d. after May 1700, Quebec province)

Louis Jolliet (or Joliet) was a French Canadian explorer and cartographer who, with the Jesuit missionary Jacques Marquette, was the first European to traverse the Mississippi River from its confluence with the Wisconsin River to the mouth of the Arkansas River in Arkansas. Jolliet received a Jesuit education in New France (now in Canada) but left his seminary in 1667 and went to France. The following year he returned to New France to work in the fur trade.

In 1672 he was commissioned by the governor of New France to explore the Mississippi, and he was joined by Marquette. On May 17, 1673, the party set out in two birchbark canoes from Michilimackinac (present-day St. Ignace, Michigan) for Green Bay, on Lake Michigan. Continuing up the Fox River in what is now central Wisconsin and down the Wisconsin River, they entered the Mississippi near present-day Prairie du Chien about a month later. Pausing along the way to make notes, to hunt, and to glean scraps of information from Indians, they arrived in July at the Quapaw Indian village (40 miles [65 km] north of present Arkansas City, Arkansas) at the mouth of the Arkansas River. From personal observations and from information given to them by the friendly Quapaw Indians, they concluded that the

Mississippi flowed south into the Gulf of Mexico—not, as they had hoped, into the Pacific Ocean. In July the party returned homeward via the Illinois River and Green Bay. Their journey is described in Marquette's journal, which has survived.

Jolliet later traveled to Hudson Bay, the Labrador coast, and a number of Canadian rivers. In 1697 he was made royal hydrographer of New France.

Henri de Tonty

(b. 1650?, Gaeta [Italy]—d. September 1704, Fort Louis, Louisiana [now in Alabama, U.S.])

The Italian-born explorer and colonizer Henri de Tonty (or Tonti) was a companion of René-Robert Cavelier, sieur de La Salle, during La Salle's North American explorations. Henri, the son of Lorenzo de Tonti, the Neapolitan financier who devised the tontine life insurance plan, joined the French army in 1668. Nine years later he lost his right hand in combat, and thereafter he wore an iron hand covered by a glove.

In 1678 the Prince de Conti recommended him to La Salle, who needed assistance in his North American explorations. Tonty became La Salle's devoted lieutenant, accompanying him on his return to his seignory (landholding) at Fort Frontenac (present-day Kingston, Ontario) and overseeing construction of the *Griffon*, the first ship to sail the upper Great Lakes. Tonty sailed on the *Griffon* for part of a westward journey, ultimately joining La Salle at the St. Joseph River (just southeast of Lake Michigan).

He subsequently helped La Salle build Fort Crèvecoeur (present-day Peoria, Illinois) during the winter of 1679–80, and he was left in charge of the Illinois region when La Salle departed for Canada in the spring. Tonty was deserted by his men and was thus unable to defend the area from marauding Iroquois, but, although wounded by their warriors, he and five survivors reached the safety of Green Bay in late 1680.

Tonty recuperated from his wounds, and in June 1681 he rejoined La Salle at Michilimackinac (present-day St. Ignace, Michigan). The two then led an expedition southward that established a settlement at Fort St. Louis on the Illinois River. The next year, Tonty and La Salle explored the Mississippi River to its mouth, claiming the area for France. La Salle left Tonty in the Illinois country when he departed for France in 1683 to gather colonists for his ill-fated Louisiana venture. Three years later, Tonty led an unsuccessful expedition down the Mississippi River in a vain search for his missing commander. He then returned to Illinois to assist in colonization and fur trading. In 1700 he joined the Louisiana settlement of Pierre Le Moyne, sieur d'Iberville, and served him faithfully until his death.

WILLIAM DAMPIER

(b. August 1651, East Coker, Somerset, England—d. March 1715, London)

William Dampier was an English buccaneer who later explored parts of the coasts of Australia,

New Guinea, and New Britain for the British Admiralty. A keen observer of natural phenomena, he was, in some respects, a pioneer in scientific exploration.

Dampier, orphaned at the age of 16, voyaged to Newfoundland and later sailed to the East Indies (Indonesia) and to the Gulf of Mexico. Between 1678 and 1691 he was engaged in piracy, chiefly along the west coast of South America and in the Pacific Ocean. On one voyage he reached Australia (1688), probably the north coast near Melville Island. He found nothing to plunder, however, and took a dislike to the Aboriginal people and their customs.

Little is known of his life for the next 10 years, until he was appointed to command of the *Roebuck* to explore for the British Admiralty. He sailed from England on January 14, 1699, rounded the Cape of Good Hope, and reached Shark Bay off western Australia on July 26. After exploring the coast northward to what was thereafter called Dampier Archipelago, he went on to New Guinea and, passing around the north of the island, reached New Britain. With a deteriorating ship and a discontented crew, he then continued to Batavia, Java (now Jakarta, Indonesia), for repairs and provisions. He sailed for England on October 17, 1700, but, by the time he reached the South Atlantic off Ascension Island on February 22, the dangerously leaking *Roebuck* had to be abandoned. The crew remained on the island until April 3, when they were picked up by a convoy of homeward-bound warships and East Indiamen. After returning to England, Dampier made two more voyages as a privateer, capturing booty worth about £200,000 on the second venture. His popular book, *A New Voyage Round the World*, was published in 1697. One of his ship's logs contains the earliest known European description of a typhoon.

Henry Kelsey

(b. c. 1667, East Greenwich, near London, England—buried November 2, 1724, East Greenwich)

The British mariner and explorer of the Canadian plains Henry Kelsey played a significant role in the establishment of the Hudson's Bay Company.

Kelsey was apprenticed to the Hudson's Bay Company (chartered 1670) by 1684, and in a trip to the region begun that year he conducted some exploration along the west shore of Hudson Bay. In 1689 he journeyed with a small party to the Churchill River area. Kelsey became proficient in Indian languages, and in 1690 he headed a company venturing ever farther westward to promote trade with the Indians and got to the Saskatchewan River and beyond. That two-year venture is believed to have made him the first European to explore Canada's central plains. Twice, incursions by the French led to the capture of the western British outpost York Fort (now York Factory, Manitoba) while he was in the fort, and both times it was he who negotiated the surrender. For several years he was master of a frigate plying Hudson Bay in trade with Native Americans. Kelsey was overseas governor of the Hudson's Bay Company from 1718 to 1722. Inexplicably, he wrote portions of many of his reports in rhyme.

Vitus Bering

(b. 1681, Horsens, Denmark—d. December 19, 1741, Bering Island, near the Kamchatka Peninsula)

Vitus Jonassen Bering was a Danish navigator whose exploration of the Bering Strait and Alaska prepared the way for a Russian foothold on the North American continent.

After a voyage to the East Indies (Indonesia), Bering joined the fleet of Tsar Peter I the Great as a sublieutenant. In 1724 the tsar appointed him leader of an expedition to determine whether Asia and North America were connected by land because Russia was interested both in colonial expansion in North America and in finding a northeast passage—i.e., a sea route to China around Siberia. (In 1648 a Russian, Semyon Dezhnyov, had sailed through the Bering Strait, but his report went unnoticed until 1736.) On July 13, 1728, Bering set sail from the Siberian peninsula of Kamchatka and in August passed through the Bering Strait into the Arctic Ocean. Bad weather prevented thorough observation, and, though he did not sight the North American coast, he concluded that Siberia and America were not joined.

During the reign of Empress Anna, Bering sought to undertake a second expedition. His simple plan, however, was expanded into Russia's Great Northern Expedition (1733–43), which mapped much of the Arctic coast of Siberia. On June 4, 1741, Bering sailed from Kamchatka in

The expedition of Vitus Bering battling adverse weather conditions while sailing through the Bering Sea. Three Lions/Hulton Archive/Getty Images

the *St. Peter*, joined by Aleksey Chirikov commanding the *St. Paul*. A storm later separated the ships, and Chirikov went on to discover several Aleutian Islands independently. Bering sailed into the Gulf of Alaska on August 20. Anxious to get his ship back to safety, he was able to reconnoitre only the southwestern coast, the Alaska Peninsula, and the Aleutian Islands. Suffering from scurvy, he was unable to maintain effective command, and the ship was wrecked early in November on the shore of Bering Island, near Kamchatka. After his death there, a few survivors were able to reach Siberia and brought news of excellent fur-trading possibilities in the Aleutians and Alaska.

Pierre Gaultier de Varennes et de La Vérendrye

(b. November 17, 1685, Trois-Rivières, New France [now Canada]—
d. December 5, 1749, Montreal)

Pierre Gaultier de Varennes et de La Vérendrye was a French-Canadian soldier, fur trader, and explorer whose exploits, little honoured during his lifetime, rank him as one of the greatest explorers of the Canadian West. Moreover, the string of trading posts he and his sons built in the course of their search for an overland route to the "western sea" broke the monopoly of the London-based Hudson's Bay Company and strengthened, for a while, French claims in North America.

La Vérendrye joined the army at the age of 12, took part in a French-Indian raid on Deerfield, Massachusetts, in 1704, and fought for France in Europe during the War of the Spanish Succession. Taken prisoner at the Battle of Malplaquet (1709), he was freed and returned to New France, where in 1726 he became a fur trader at Lake Nipigon, 35 miles (56 km) north of Lake Superior. From the Native Americans he heard of a great river that might lead to the Pacific Ocean and thence to the riches of East Asia. To discover the secrets of the West, he and his sons built a string of trading posts between 1731 and 1738 reaching from what is now Rainy Lake in Ontario (Fort-Saint-Pierre) to Winnipeg (Fort-Rouge) in present-day

Manitoba. To these convenient posts Native Americans brought their furs and gave La Vérendrye crude maps of waterways they said would lead him to the "western sea."

In the fall of 1738 La Vérendrye reached the Mandan Indian villages on the Missouri River in what is now North Dakota, and in 1742 he sent two of his sons to push beyond the Missouri. It is possible that they penetrated the region now occupied by Nebraska, Montana, and Wyoming and perhaps saw, but did not cross, the Rocky Mountains. On the return journey, they paused near present-day Pierre, South Dakota, where on March 30, 1743, they placed a lead tablet, claiming the country for France.

Despite having sent some 30,000 beaver pelts to Quebec annually (most of which would normally have gone to the rival Hudson's Bay Company) and having pushed farther west than any other person of European descent, entirely at his own expense, La Vérendrye was severely criticized by French government authorities for failing to find the western sea and was blamed for the deaths of one of his sons, a nephew, and a Roman Catholic priest at the hands of hostile Native Americans. Old and ill, he still pressed for another chance to explore the West. Permission was finally granted, but he died before he could leave Montreal.

Charles-Marie de La Condamine

(b. January 28, 1701, Paris, France—d. February 4, 1774, Paris)

The French naturalist, mathematician, and adventurer Charles-Marie de La Condamine is best known for accomplishing the first scientific exploration of the Amazon River.

After finishing his basic education in Paris, La Condamine embarked on a military career. He left the army for a brief stint (1730–31) of scientific study at the Academy of Sciences in Paris before leaving in May 1731 for what became a year-long sea voyage to various ports in the Mediterranean. Returning to Paris, he reported his scientific observations to the academy, which was sufficiently impressed to invite him to join an expedition to Peru to determine the length near the Equator of a degree of the meridian.

The party, which also included French scientist Pierre Bouguer, left in April 1735 and finally arrived at its destination, Quito (now in Ecuador), in June 1736. The project was fraught with delays and dissension among the participants and was not completed until 1743. In May La Condamine left the party, deciding to return to France via the Amazon, and began a four-month raft journey down to the river's mouth. During the trip he made a number of geographic, astronomic, biologic, and ethnographic observations of the regions through which he passed, and he continued such documentation in Cayenne, French Guiana, while he waited for a ship home. He finally reached Paris in early 1745. Two plant genera that were of particular interest to him during his time in South America were *Hevea* (the source of natural rubber) and *Cinchona* (the source of quinine), both of which were little known in Europe at that time. In addition to a scientific account of his journey, he published *Journal du voyage fait par ordre du roi a l'équateur* (1751; "Journal of a Voyage to the Equator Made by Order of the King").

John Byron

(b. November 8, 1723, England?—d. April 10, 1786, England)

John Byron was a British admiral and explorer whose account (1768) of a shipwreck in South America was to some extent used by his grandson, the poet Lord Byron, in *Don Juan*.

The second son of the 4th Baron Byron, he was a midshipman on board the *Wager* in 1741 when it was wrecked off the coast of Chile during George Anson's voyage around the world. After unparalleled hardships Byron eventually reached a Spanish prison and was repatriated in 1745. He was appointed to the command of the frigate *Dolphin* in 1764 and sent out to the Pacific Ocean in an attempt to discover the supposed southern continent, but he made only a fruitless circumnavigation lasting 22 months. Appointed governor of Newfoundland in 1769, he reached flag rank in 1775 and became vice admiral in 1778.

In 1779 he lived up to his nickname "Foul-weather Jack" when, in command of a fleet sent to relieve British forces in America, he encountered one of the worst Atlantic gales on record. It is to this that Lord Byron alludes in his "Epistle to Augusta":

A strange doom is thy father's son's, and past

Recalling, as it lies beyond redress;

Reversed for him our grandsire's fate of yore,

He had no rest at sea, nor I on shore.

As commander in chief of the West Indies, John Byron fought an inconclusive battle with Charles-Hector, count d'Estaing, off Grenada in 1779.

James Cook

(b. October 27, 1728, Marton-in-Cleveland, Yorkshire, England—d. February 14, 1779, Kealakekua Bay, Hawaii)

The renowned British naval captain and navigator James Cook was the greatest explorer of his day. Over a period of two decades he explored the seaways and coasts of Canada (1759, 1763–67) and conducted three expeditions to the Pacific Ocean (1768–71; 1772–75; 1776–79), ranging from the Antarctic ice fields to the Bering Strait and from the coasts of North America to Australia and New Zealand.

EARLY LIFE

James Cook was the son of a farmhand migrant from Scotland. While Cook was still a child, his father became the foreman on a farm in a neighbouring village. Young James early showed signs of an inquiring and able mind,

James Cook. Photos.com/Thinkstock

and his father's employer paid for his schooling in the village until he was 12 years old. His early teens were spent on the farm where his father worked, but a brief apprenticeship in a general store in a coastal village north of Whitby brought him in contact with ships and the sea. At the age of 18, in 1746, he was apprenticed to a well-known Quaker shipowner, John Walker of Whitby, and at 21 was rated able seaman in the Walker collier-barks—stout, seaworthy, slow 300- and 400-ton craft mainly used in the North Sea trade. When the ships were laid up for refitting (done by the apprentices and crews) at Whitby during the worst months of winter, Cook lived ashore and studied mathematics by night. The Whitby barks, constantly working North Sea waters off a dangerous and ill-marked lee shore, offered Cook splendid practical training: the young man who learned his seamanship there had little to fear from any other sea.

Promoted to mate in 1752, Cook was offered command of a bark three years later, after eight years at sea. Advancement of this nature opened up a career that would have satisfied most working seamen, but instead Cook volunteered as able seaman in the Royal Navy. The navy, he was sure, offered a more interesting career for the competent professional seaman, and greater opportunity than in the North Sea barks. Tall, of striking appearance, Cook almost immediately caught the attention of his superiors, and with excellent power of command, he was marked for rapid advancement.

After advancing to master's mate, and boatswain, both noncommissioned ranks, he was made master of HMS *Pembroke* at the age of 29. During the Seven Years' War between Great Britain and France (1756–63) he saw action in the Bay of Biscay, was given command of a captured ship, and took part in the siege of Louisburg in Nova Scotia and in the successful amphibious assault against Quebec. His charting and marking of the more difficult reaches of the St. Lawrence River contributed to the success of General Wolfe's landing there. Based at Halifax during the winters, he mastered surveying with the plane table. Between 1763 and 1768, after the war had ended, he commanded the schooner *Grenville* while surveying the coasts of Newfoundland, sailing most of the year and working on his charts at his base in England during the winters. In 1766 he observed an eclipse of the Sun and sent the details to the Royal Society in London—an unusual activity for a noncommissioned officer, for Cook still rated only as master.

VOYAGES AND DISCOVERIES

In 1768 the Royal Society, in conjunction with the Admiralty, was organizing the first scientific expedition to the Pacific, and the rather obscure 40-year-old James Cook was appointed commander of the expedition. Hurriedly commissioned as lieutenant, he was given a homely looking but extremely sturdy Whitby coal-hauling bark renamed HMS *Endeavour*, then four years old, of just 368 tons, and less than 98 feet (30 metres) long. Cook's orders were to convey gentlemen of the Royal Society and their assistants to Tahiti to observe the transit of the planet Venus across the Sun. That done, on June 3, 1769, he was to find the southern continent, the so-called Terra Australis, which philosophers argued must exist to balance the landmasses of the Northern Hemisphere. The leader of the scientists was the rich and able Joseph Banks, aged 26, who was assisted by Daniel Solander, a Swedish botanist, as well as astronomers (Cook rating as one) and artists. Cook carried an early nautical almanac and brass sextants, but no chronometer on the first voyage.

Striking south and southwest from Tahiti, where his predecessors had sailed west and west-northwest with the favouring trade winds, Cook found and charted all of New Zealand, a difficult job that took six months. After that, instead of turning before the west winds for the homeward run around Cape Horn, he crossed the Tasman Sea westward and, on April 19, 1770, came on the southeast coast of Australia. Running north along its 2,000-mile (3,200-km) eastern coast, surveying as he went, Cook successfully navigated Queensland's Great Barrier Reef—since reckoned as one of the greatest navigational hazards in the world—taking the Coral Sea and the Torres Strait in his stride. Once the bark touched on a coral spur by night, but it withstood the impact and was refloated. After the *Endeavour* was grounded on the nearby Queensland coast and repaired, Cook sailed it back to England. He stopped briefly at Batavia (modern Jakarta, Indonesia) for supplies, and, although the crew had been remarkably healthy until then, 30 died of fever and dysentery contracted while on land. None of the crew, however, died of scurvy (a dietary disease caused by a lack of ascorbic acid [vitamin C] that habitually decimated the crews of ships on lengthy voyages in the 18th century). This was because, in addition to ensuring cleanliness and ventilation in the crew's quarters, Cook insisted on an appropriate diet that included cress, sauerkraut, and a kind of orange extract. The health in which he maintained his sailors in consequence made his name a naval byword.

Back in England, he was promoted to commander and presented to King George III, and soon he began to organize another and even more ambitious voyage. The success of the expedition of Joseph Banks and his scientists (which established the useful principle of sending scientists on naval voyages—e.g., Charles Darwin in the *Beagle*, T.H. Huxley in the *Rattlesnake*, and J.D. Hooker with Sir James Ross to the Ross Sea in the Antarctic) stimulated interest not only in the discovery of new lands but in the new knowledge in many other scientific subjects. The wealth of scientifically collected material from the *Endeavour* voyage was unique. Cook was now sent out with two ships to make the first circumnavigation of and penetration into the Antarctic.

Between July 1772 and July 1775 Cook made what ranks as one of the greatest sailing ship voyages, again with a small former Whitby ship, the *Resolution*, and a consort ship, the *Adventure*. He found no trace of Terra Australis, though he sailed beyond latitude 70° S in the Antarctic, but he successfully completed the first west-east circumnavigation in high latitudes, charted Tonga and Easter Island during the winters, and discovered New Caledonia in the Pacific and the South Sandwich Islands and South Georgia Island in the Atlantic. He showed that a real Terra Australis existed only in the landmasses of Australia, New Zealand, and whatever land might remain frozen beyond the ice rim of Antarctica. And, once again, not one of his crew died of scurvy. Back in England, he was promoted to captain at last, elected a fellow of the Royal Society, and awarded one of its highest honours, the gold Copley Medal, for a paper that he prepared on his work against scurvy.

There was yet one secret of the Pacific to be discovered: whether there existed a Northwest Passage around Canada and Alaska or a Northeast one around Siberia, between the Atlantic and Pacific oceans. Although the passages had long been sought in vain from Europe, it was thought that the search from the North Pacific might be successful. The man to undertake the search obviously was Cook, and in July 1776 he went off again on the *Resolution* with another Whitby ship, the *Discovery*. This search was unsuccessful, for neither a Northwest nor a Northeast Passage usable by sailing ships existed, and the voyage

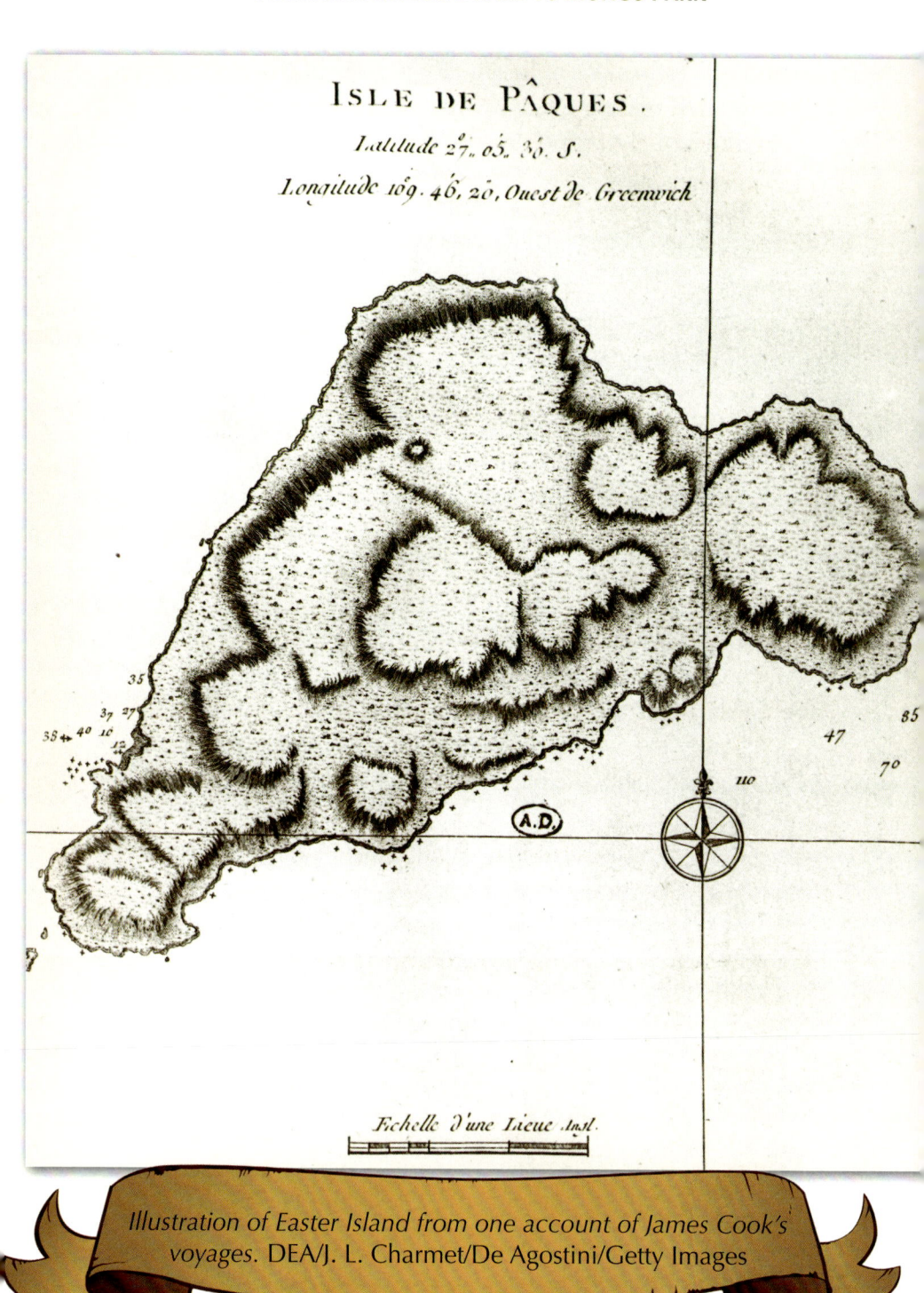

Illustration of Easter Island from one account of James Cook's voyages. DEA/J. L. Charmet/De Agostini/Getty Images

led to Cook's death. In a brief fracas with Hawaiians over the stealing of a cutter, Cook was slain on the beach at Kealakekua by the Polynesian inhabitants.

Cook's voyaging left him comparatively little time for family life. Although Cook had married Elizabeth Batts in 1762, when he was 34 years old, he was at sea for more than half of their married life. The couple had six children, three of whom died in infancy. The three surviving sons, two of whom entered the navy, had all died by 1794.

Cook had set new standards of thoroughness in discovery and seamanship, in navigation, cartography, and the sea care of men, in relations with natives both friendly and hostile, and in the application of science at sea; moreover he had peacefully changed the map of the world more than any other single man in history.

Louis-Antoine de Bougainville

(b. November 11, 1729, Paris, France—d. August 31, 1811, Paris)

The great French navigator Louis-Antoine de Bougainville explored areas of the South Pacific as leader of the first French naval force to sail around the world (1766–69). His widely read account, *Voyage autour du monde* (1771; *A Voyage Round the World*, 1772), helped popularize a belief in the moral worth of people in their natural state, a concept of considerable significance in the French thought of his day.

Louis-Antoine de Bouganiville. Apic/Hulton Fine Art Collection/Getty Images

Louis-Antoine de Bougainville

Entering the army at age 24, Bougainville went to Canada (1756) as aide-de-camp to General Louis-Joseph de Montcalm and distinguished himself against the British in the French and Indian War. Having left the army for the navy in 1763, he voyaged the next year into the Atlantic Ocean near the tip of South America to establish a colony for France in the Falkland Islands. The colony was ceded to Spain in 1767.

Commissioned by the French government to circle Earth in a voyage of exploration, Bougainville put to sea in December 1766, accompanied by naturalists and other scientists. After passing through the Strait of Magellan, he went northwest through the South Pacific and visited Tahiti. Sailing west, he touched Samoa and the New Hebrides and then continued west into waters not previously navigated by any European ship. He proved that Espiritu Santo was an island and not part of the rumoured southern continent of Terra Australis Incognita. On the fringes of the Great Barrier Reef, he turned north without sighting Australia, passed the edge of the Solomon Islands, and went on to New Britain in the Bismarck Archipelago. Because his men were by then suffering from scurvy, and the ships needed refitting, he stopped at Buru in the Moluccas (September 1768) and at Batavia (now Jakarta) in Java. He returned to Saint-Malo, in Brittany, in March 1769, having lost seven men.

Bougainville became secretary to Louis XV (1772) and served as chef d'escadre (commodore) in operations of the French fleet off North America (1779–82) in support of the American Revolution. After a French defeat off Martinique (April 12, 1782), he was court-martialed. During the French Revolution, he escaped the massacres of Paris in 1792 and settled on his estate in Normandy. Napoleon I made him a senator, count, and member of the

Legion of Honour. Named for him are the largest of the Solomon Islands, a strait in the New Hebrides group, and the plant genus *Bougainvillea*.

JAMES BRUCE

(b. December 14, 1730, Larbert, Stirling, Scotland—d. April 27, 1794, Larbert)

James Bruce was a Scottish explorer who, in the course of daring travels in Ethiopia, reached the headstream of the Blue Nile River, then thought to be the Nile River's main source. The credibility of his observations, published in *Travels to Discover the Source of the Nile* (1790), was questioned in Britain, partly because he had first told the French court of his discoveries. Reports by later travelers, however, confirmed the accuracy of his account.

As British consul (1763 and afterward) in Algiers (Algeria), Bruce studied many antiquities of North Africa, recording what he saw in fine drawings. Beginning in 1765 he traveled widely in the Mediterranean region, notably in Syria, and arrived at Alexandria, Egypt, in July 1768. Intent on reaching the source of the Nile, he left Cairo on an arduous journey by way of the Nile, Aswān, the Red Sea, and Mitsiwa (now Massawa, Eritrea), eventually reaching the Ethiopian capital of Gonder on February 14, 1770.

Despite serious political unrest in Ethiopia, Bruce continued his expedition and reached Lake Tana, where the Blue Nile rises, on November 14. The journey homeward was one of extreme hardship. He arrived at Marseille, France, in March 1773 and returned to London in 1774. Following retirement to his estate, he began writing in 1780 a vivid account of his travels, considered one of the epics of African adventure literature.

Carsten Niebuhr

(b. March 17, 1733, Lüdingworth, Hanover [Germany]—d. April 26, 1815, Meldorf, Holstein)

Carsten Niebuhr was a German surveyor and traveler who was the sole survivor of the first scientific expedition to Arabia and the compiler of its results.

He learned surveying and in 1760 was invited to join the Arabian expedition being sent out by Frederick V of Denmark. The party visited the Nile, Mount Sinai, Suez, and Jidda, the port of Mecca, and then went overland to Mocha (al-Mukhā) in southwestern Arabia. The death of the expedition's philologist (May 1763) was followed by that of the naturalist in July. The remaining party members visited Sanaa, the capital of Yemen, and returned to Mocha. The group then sailed for Bombay (now Mumbai, India), where the artist and the surgeon of the expedition died, leaving Niebuhr alone. He stayed 14 months in India and then turned homeward by way of Muscat (in southeastern Arabia), Persia (Iran), Mesopotamia, Cyprus, and Asia Minor (Turkey), reaching Copenhagen, Denmark, in November 1767.

He wrote *Beschreibung von Arabien* (1772; "Description of Arabia") and *Reisebeschreibung nach Arabien und andern umliegenden Ländern* (1774; "Travels Through Arabia").

Daniel Boone

(b. *c.* November 2, 1734, Berks County, Pennsylvania [U.S.]—d. *c.* September 26, 1820, St. Charles County, Missouri, U.S.)

The early American frontiersman and legendary hero Daniel Boone helped blaze a trail through Cumberland Gap, a notch in the Appalachian Mountains near the juncture of Virginia, Tennessee, and Kentucky. He had little formal schooling but learned to read and write. As a youth he moved with his family (English Quakers) to the Yadkin River Valley region on the North Carolina frontier. Most of his life was spent as a wandering hunter and trapper. He reached as far south as Florida and at least as far west as present-day Missouri and possibly Nebraska during his travels.

Many white people had traversed Kentucky before Boone; hence, the legend that he was its discoverer needs qualification. Boone first went a short way through Cumberland Gap to hunt in the fall of 1767, and he and several companions returned to Kentucky to trap and hunt in 1769–71. He returned to North Carolina with little material gain, but he had acquired considerable knowledge of the Kentucky and north-central Tennessee region in his explorations. In 1773 Boone undertook to lead his own and several other families to Kentucky, but the group was attacked by Cherokee Indians just beyond the last settlement. Two of the party, including Boone's son James, were captured, tortured, and murdered, whereupon the survivors turned back.

In March 1775 Boone and 28 companions were employed by Richard Henderson's Transylvania Company to blaze a trail through Cumberland Gap. The company planned to establish Kentucky as a 14th colony. Despite Indian attacks, the party built the Wilderness Road, which ran from eastern Virginia into the interior of Kentucky

Daniel Boone leading settlers through the Cumberland Gap. MPI/Archive Photos/Getty Images

and beyond and became the main route to the region then known as the West. It helped make possible the immediate opening of the first settlements in Kentucky: Boonesborough, Harrod's Town, and Benjamin Logan's. In August 1775 Boone brought his wife, Rebecca, and their daughter to Boonesborough. They were, except for a few women who had been captured by Indians, the first white women in Kentucky, and their arrival may be said to mark the first permanent settlement there. The plan to establish the 14th colony failed, however, and Kentucky was made a county of Virginia.

Boone became a captain in the county's militia during the American Revolution and a leader in defending Boonesborough against the Indians. In July 1776 he led a group of settlers who were able to rescue, unharmed, his daughter and two other girls who had been captured by Indians three days earlier. News of that incident greatly enhanced his reputation. He was captured by Indians in early 1778 and was adopted as a son by the Shawnee chief Blackfish. After five months he escaped to warn Boonesborough settlers of an impending attack. When the attack by British soldiers and Indians came (September 1778), the vastly outnumbered defenders of the settlement successfully withstood a 10-day siege.

Although a courageous and resourceful leader, Boone did not prosper. He established extensive land claims but could rarely make them good. After the revolution he worked as a surveyor along the Ohio River. He settled for a few years in Kanawha County, Virginia (now West Virginia). Then, in 1799, he and members of his family (including son Nathan Boone) followed his son Daniel Morgan Boone to Missouri, in Louisiana Territory (then belonging to Spain), where he continued to hunt and trap. He died at Nathan's home west of St. Louis and not far from the Missouri River.

A legendary hero even at the time of his death, Boone's fame spread worldwide when in 1823 Lord Byron devoted seven stanzas to him in his long satiric poem *Don Juan*. He has been the subject of other works of literature (fiction and biography), paintings, and dramatic productions, including a long-running (1964–70) television series. His name has been preserved in a variety of geographic names in the United States in addition to Boonesborough, including Boone, North Carolina. The Daniel Boone Homestead in southeastern Pennsylvania, about 9 miles (14 km) southeast of Reading, preserves structures associated with Boone's birthplace, and Nathan Boone's house in Missouri is also a historical site.

Arthur Phillip

(b. October 11, 1738, London, England—d. August 31, 1814, Bath, Somerset)

The British admiral Arthur Phillip led the expedition that in 1788 established a convict settlement at what is now Sydney. This was the first permanent European colony on the Australian continent.

Phillip joined the British Navy in 1755, retired in 1763 to farm for 13 years in England, then served with the Portuguese Navy against Spain (1776) and with the British Navy against France (1778). In 1786 he was assigned the duty of founding a British convict settlement in New South Wales, and the following year he set sail with 11 ships.

As the first governor of New South Wales, Phillip struggled with rebellious convicts and troops and—until mid-1790—with the threat of famine; but he successfully created a permanent community. Despite his conciliatory policy toward the native Aborigines, he failed to establish peace between the settlers and the local people. He returned to England in 1792 because of poor health, but he saw further action at sea (1796–98) and was promoted to admiral in 1814.

Jean-François de Galaup, comte de La Pérouse

(b. August 22, 1741, near Albi, France—
d. c. 1788)

The French naval officer and navigator Jean-François de Galaup, comte de La Pérouse, is known for the wide-ranging explorations in the Pacific Ocean that he conducted in the later half of the 1780s.

La Pérouse joined the French navy while in his teens and gradually became an accomplished navigator and seaman. By 1780 he was a captain, and, with France having taken the side of the United States during the American Revolution, he commanded a successful campaign against British settlements on the shore of Hudson Bay (1782). In 1783, following the conclusion of the war, France began preparations to send an expedition to the Pacific to continue the

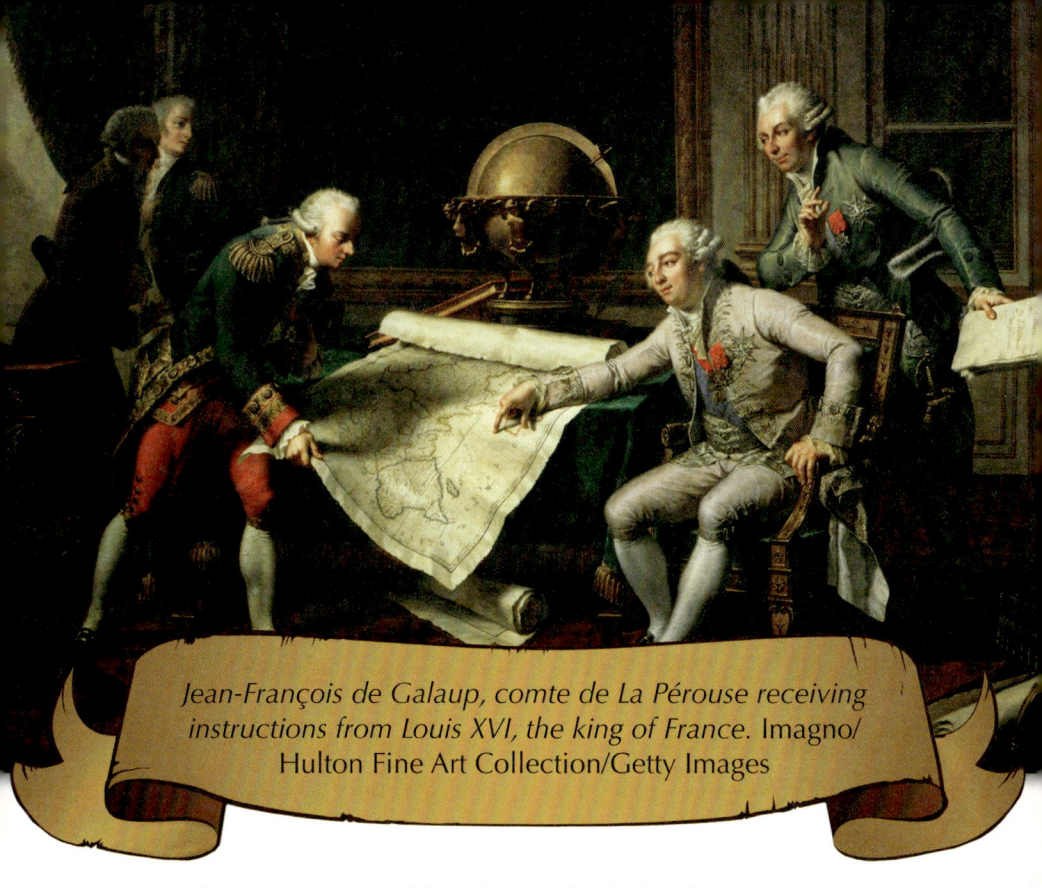

Jean-François de Galaup, comte de La Pérouse receiving instructions from Louis XVI, the king of France. Imagno/Hulton Fine Art Collection/Getty Images

explorations started by James Cook in the previous two decades. La Pérouse was made leader of the expedition.

With La Pérouse commanding the ship *La Boussole* and accompanied by the *Astrolabe*, the explorers sailed from France on August 1, 1785. After rounding Cape Horn, La Pérouse made a stop in the South Pacific at Easter Island (April 9, 1786). Investigating tropical Pacific waters, he visited the Sandwich Islands (now Hawaii) and, with the object of locating the Northwest Passage from the Pacific, he made his way to North America. He reached the southern shore of Alaska, near Mount St. Elias, in June 1786 and explored the western coast of North America southward beyond San Francisco to Monterey. He then crossed the Pacific and reached the South China coast at Macau on January 3, 1787. Leaving Manila (Philippines) on April 9, he began to explore the Pacific coast of Asia. He sailed through the Sea of Japan

(East Sea) up to the Tatar Strait, which separates the mainland from the island of Sakhalin, and also visited the strait, subsequently named for him, that separates Sakhalin from the island of Hokkaido, Japan. At Petropavlovsk on the Siberian peninsula of Kamchatka, he dispatched his expedition journal and maps overland to France. The ships then made for the Navigators' (now Samoa) Islands, where the commander of the *Astrolabe* and 11 of his men were murdered. La Pérouse then went to the Friendly (now Tonga) and Norfolk islands on his way to Botany Bay in eastern Australia, from which he departed on March 10, 1788.

Nothing more was known of him until 1826–27, when the English captain-adventurer Peter Dillon found evidence that *La Boussole* and the *Astrolabe* had been near Vanikoro, one of the Santa Cruz Islands (now in Solomon Islands). In 1828 the French explorer Dumont d'Urville sighted wreckage and learned from islanders that about 30 men from the ships had been massacred on shore, though others who were well armed managed to escape. La Pérouse's records, *Voyage de La Pérouse autour du monde*, 4 vol. (1797; *A Voyage Round the World*), were edited by L.A. Milet-Mureau and published posthumously.

Sir Joseph Banks, Baronet

(b. February 13, 1743, London, England—d. June 19, 1820, Isleworth, London)

Sir Joseph Banks was a British explorer, naturalist, and long-time president of the Royal Society, known for his promotion of science.

Banks was schooled at Harrow School and Eton College before attending Christ Church College, Oxford, from 1760 to 1763; he inherited a considerable fortune from his father in 1761. Banks then traveled extensively, collecting plant and natural history specimens in journeys to Newfoundland and Labrador (1766), around the world with Captain James Cook (1768–71), and to Iceland (1772).

Banks was interested in economic plants and their introduction into countries. He was the first to suggest (1805) the identity of the wheat rust and barberry fungus, and he was the first to show that marsupial mammals were more primitive than placental mammals. In his capacity as honorary director of the Royal Botanic Gardens at Kew (near London), he sent many botanical collectors to various countries. His house became a meeting place for the exchange of ideas. After he became president of the Royal Society (1778–1820), he improved the position of science in Britain and cultivated interchange with scientists of other nations; he was, however, accused by many fellow scientists of exercising excessive authority as president and even of being "despotic." In 1781 he was made a baronet. The order of Knight Commander of the Bath was bestowed upon him in 1795, and two years later he was admitted to the Privy Council.

Banks's herbarium, considered one of the most important in existence, and his library, a major collection of works on natural history, are now at the British Museum. *Banks' Florilegium*, a collection of engravings of plants compiled by Banks and based on drawings by Swedish botanist Daniel Solander during Cook's 1768–71 voyage, was not published in full until 1989.

Samuel Hearne

(b. 1745, London, England—d. November 1792, England)

The English seaman, fur trader, and explorer Samuel Hearne was the first European to make an overland trip to the Arctic Ocean. He was also the first to show the trend of the Arctic shore.

Samuel Hearne. Hulton Archive/Getty Images

At the age of 11, Hearne became a midshipman in the British Royal Navy. From 1766 he worked for the British-based Hudson's Bay Company as mate on company vessels, one of which took him in 1769 to Prince of Wales Fort at the mouth of the Churchill River (near present-day Churchill, Manitoba), Canada.

Between the fort and the Arctic Ocean lay an immense region known only as the Barren Grounds, rumoured to be filled with riches, including copper. It was speculated that the mysterious tundra even offered a route to Asia. Twice frustrated in attempts to explore the territory for the Hudson's Bay Company, Hearne left the Churchill River in December 1770, accompanied only by an Indian guide and the guide's eight wives. The following July he found the mouth of the river that he is said to have named the Coppermine (in present-day Northwest Territories and Nunavut). When he returned to the fort in June 1772, he had walked some 5,000 miles (8,000 km) and explored more than 250,000 square miles (650,000 square km).

In 1774 Hearne built for the Hudson's Bay Company its first interior trading post, Cumberland House, on the Saskatchewan River, the first permanent settlement in what is now Saskatchewan. He was serving the Hudson's Bay Company as governor and was in command of Prince of Wales Fort in 1782 when the French plundered and destroyed the fort and took Hearne prisoner.

To the credit of the French navy, Hearne was treated with dignity. The French commander Jean-François de Galaup, comte de La Pérouse, himself an explorer, encouraged Hearne not only to preserve his papers but also to publish an account of his fabulous journey to the Arctic. Released by the French, Hearne spent four relatively uneventful years in Canada (1783–87) before he returned to England to write *A Journey from Prince of Wales's Fort in Hudson's Bay to the Northern Ocean in the Years 1769, 1770,*

1771, & 1772 (published posthumously, 1795, with numerous new editions and reprintings).

Georg Forster

(b. November 26, 1754, Nassenhuben, near Danzig [now Gdansk], Poland—d. January 12, 1794, Paris, France)

The German explorer and scientist Johann Georg Adam Forster is best known for helping to establish the literary travel book as a favoured genre in German literature.

With his father, Johann Reinhold Forster, he emigrated to England in 1766. Both were invited to accompany Captain James Cook on his second voyage around the world (1772–75). Georg Forster's account of the journey, *A Voyage Towards the South Pole and Round the World* (1777), was based on his father's journals; it later appeared in a German version, *Reise um die Welt* (1778–80). A work of travel, science, and literature, the book not only established Forster as one of the most accomplished stylists of the time but also influenced German scientific and literary writing, including that of Johann Wolfgang von Goethe, Johann Gottfried von Herder, and Alexander von Humboldt. A superb essayist, Forster contributed to the scientific, especially botanical, knowledge of the South Pacific Ocean.

He held professorships at the University of Kassel (1778–84), and at the university at Wilno (now Vilnius, Lithuania; 1784–87), before becoming librarian at the University of Mainz. Sympathetic with the French Revolution, he championed the republican government in Mainz, occupied by the French in 1792, and in 1793 he went to Paris to negotiate on its behalf. Meanwhile the Germans seized Mainz. Forster spent his final days in Paris, reviled among Germans as a traitor and disillusioned by the excesses of the Reign of Terror in France.

GEORGE VANCOUVER

(b. June 22, 1757, King's Lynn, Norfolk, England—d. May 10, 1798, Richmond, Surrey)

George Vancouver was an English navigator who, with great precision, completed one of the most difficult surveys ever undertaken, that of the Pacific coast of North America, from the vicinity of San Francisco northward to present-day British Columbia. At that time he verified that no continuous channel exists between the Pacific Ocean and Hudson Bay, in northeastern Canada.

Vancouver entered the Royal Navy at age 13 and accompanied Captain James Cook on his second and third voyages (1772–75 and 1776–80). After nine years' service in the West Indies, he took command of the expedition to the northwest coast of North America for which he is noted. Departing from England on April 1, 1791, he went by way of the Cape of Good Hope to Australia, where

Statue of George Vancouver in King's Lynn, Eng., where Vancouver was born. Graham Taylor/Shutterstock.com

he surveyed part of the southwest coast. After stops at Tahiti and the Hawaiian Islands, Vancouver sighted the west coast of North America at latitude 39°27′ N on April 17, 1792. He examined the coast with minute care, surveying the intricate inlets and channels in the region of Vancouver Island and naming, among others, Puget Sound and the Gulf of Georgia. By August he was negotiating with the Spaniards to take control of their former coastal station at Nootka Sound, off Vancouver Island. Continuing his coastal exploration in April 1793, he surveyed north to 56°44′ N and south to below present-day San Luis Obispo, California. In 1794 he sailed to Cook's Inlet, off southern Alaska, and, after a fresh survey of much of the coast north of San Francisco, sailed homeward via Cape Horn, reaching England on October 20, 1794. His *Voyage of Discovery to the North Pacific Ocean and Round the World...1790–95*, three volumes with an atlas of maps and plates, was published after his death in 1798.

Sir Alexander Mackenzie

(b. 1763/64, Stornoway, Isle of Lewis, Scotland—d. March 11/12, 1820, near Dunkeld, Scotland)

Sir Alexander Mackenzie was a Scottish fur trader and explorer who traced the course of the 1,025-mile (1,650-km) Mackenzie River in Canada.

Immigrating to North America, he entered (1779) a Montreal trading firm, which amalgamated with the North West Company, a rival of the Hudson's Bay Company. In what is now the province of Alberta, Mackenzie and a cousin set up a trading post, Fort Chipewyan, on Lake Athabasca (1788). This was the starting point of his expedition of 1789, which followed the Mackenzie from the Great Slave Lake to the river's delta on the Arctic Ocean. In 1793 Mackenzie crossed the Rocky Mountains from Fort Chipewyan to the Pacific coast of what is now British Columbia. These journeys together constitute the first known transcontinental crossing of America north of Mexico. His *Voyages from Montreal, on the River St. Laurence, Through the Continent of North America, to the Frozen and Pacific Oceans; In the Years 1789 and 1793* was published in 1801. He was knighted in 1802 and lived in Scotland after 1812.

GEORGE BASS

(b. January 30, 1771, Aswarby, Lincolnshire, England—d. 1803, at sea en route from Australia to South America)

The English surgeon, sailor, and explorer George Bass was important in the early coastal survey of Australia. Bass was apprenticed as a surgeon and in 1789 accepted in the Company of Surgeons. He joined the Royal Navy, where his proficiency in navigation and seamanship and interest in Pacific exploration led to his transfer to the ship *Reliance*, on which the navigator Matthew Flinders was mate. When the ship reached Port Jackson (in what is now New South Wales) in 1795, Bass, Flinders, and Bass's personal servant William Martin explored the George's River and Botany Bay and recommended a settlement, which was made at Banks Town. In 1796 the three unsuccessfully sought a river south of Botany Bay and discovered and explored Port Hocking. Bass also studied the animals and plants of the region. In 1797 Bass explored the coast south of Sydney and confirmed reports of coal there. Later in the year and in 1798 he determined the existence of a strait—which subsequently was named for him—between New South Wales and Van Diemen's Land (now Tasmania). In 1799 Bass was elected to the Linnean Society of London for his field collections and writings.

Bass then turned to commercial ventures, although he continued to chart wherever he sailed. In 1803 he sailed with a cargo from Sydney bound for South America and was never heard from again.

Mungo Park

(b. September 10, 1771, Fowlshiels, Selkirk, Scotland—d. c. January 1806, near Bussa on the Niger River [now in Nigeria])

The Scottish explorer Mungo Park is known for his journeys in sub-Saharan West Africa, notably along the Niger River.

Mungo Park riding through a jungle in Africa. Time & Life Pictures/Getty Images

Educated as a surgeon at the University of Edinburgh, Park was appointed a medical officer in 1792 on a vessel engaged in trade with the East Indies (Indonesia). His subsequent studies of the plant and animal life of Sumatra won for him the backing of the African Association to explore the true course of the Niger River. Beginning his exploration at the mouth of the Gambia River on June 21, 1795, Park ascended that river for 200 miles (320 km) to Pisania (now Karantaba, The Gambia), a British trading station. Hampered by fever and formidable hardships, he crossed the unknown territory of the upper Sénégal River basin. He was imprisoned by an Arab chief for four months but escaped on July 1, 1796, to continue his journey with little more than a horse and a compass. On July 20 he reached Ségou (now in Mali) on the Niger, which he followed downstream for 80 miles (130 km) to Silla. Finally forced to turn back for lack of supplies, Park, traveling on foot, took a more southerly route on his return. After traversing mountainous country, he arrived at Kamalia in Mandingo country, where he lay dangerously ill with fever for seven months. With the assistance of a slave trader, he reached Pisania on June 10, 1797. He returned to Britain to write an account of his adventures, *Travels in the Interior Districts of Africa* (1797), which became a popular success and made him famous.

Two years later Park married and practiced medicine in Peebles in Scotland until asked by the government to head a second expedition to the Niger. Commissioned a captain, he led a party of 40 Europeans to Pisania and, on August 19, 1805, with only 11 survivors, reached Bamako (now in Mali) on the Niger. Resuming the journey by canoe, he and his companions reached Ségou, where the local ruler gave him permission to continue his voyage down the unexplored river. Hoping to reach the coast at the end of January 1806, he set sail with eight companions from Sansanding, a little below Ségou, on November 19, 1805. Reports that the expedition had met with disaster soon reached the settlements on the Gambia. In 1812 it was learned that when the explorers reached the rapids at Bussa, about 1,000 miles (1,600 km) below Sansanding, they were attacked by local inhabitants, and Park was drowned.

Matthew Flinders

(b. March 16, 1774, Donington, Lincolnshire, England—d. July 19, 1814, London)

Matthew Flinders was an English navigator who charted much of the Australian coast. His name has been preserved in a number of Australian geographic names, including the Flinders Ranges in South Australia.

Flinders entered the Royal Navy in 1789 and became a navigator. In 1795 he sailed to Australia, where he explored and charted its southeast coast and circumnavigated the island of Tasmania. As commander of the *Investigator*, he again sailed from England for Australia in 1801. On this visit he surveyed the entire southern coast, from Cape Leeuwin, in the southwest, to the Bass Strait, which separates mainland Australia from Tasmania. On July 22, 1802, he sailed from Sydney (on Port Jackson) and charted the east coast of Australia and the Gulf of Carpentaria on the north coast. Continuing westward and southward, he circumnavigated Australia and again reached Port Jackson on June 9, 1803.

In October, on the voyage back to England, the condition of his ship required him to stop at the Île de France (now Mauritius) in the western Indian Ocean. There he was interned by the French authorities and was not allowed to leave for England until 1810. His *Voyage to Terra Australis* appeared shortly before his death.

Conclusion

The roughly quarter of a millennium from the mid-16th to the end of the 18th century was a remarkable period in world history. In Europe, it was when the last decades of the Renaissance were merging into the era that came to be known as the Enlightenment—a time of scientific and philosophical inquiry and of remarkable technological breakthroughs. It was also an era when a cast of essentially all European men set out in great numbers to follow in the footsteps of the pioneering voyagers of the Age of Exploration of the previous century and a half. Many of the great figures in this second wave of explorers—notably Sir Francis Drake, Abel Janszoon Tasman, and James Cook—gained enough renown to rival such legendary icons as Christopher Columbus, Vasco da Gama, and Ferdinand Magellan from that earlier time.

This newer group of individuals, benefiting from advances in technology (including larger, stronger vessels and improved navigational devices) as well as from more detailed and accurate maps and nautical charts, were able to significantly expand the boundaries of the known world. Although they did not find the long-desired easy routes to Asia via the north or solve the riddle of Terra Australis Incognita—those achievements would await future generations of explorers—their great number of notable accomplishments included discovering Australasia and many of the islands of Oceania, charting the length of the North American coastline and determining that the continent was separate from Asia, and identifying many of the major features of the continental interiors of the Americas and Africa.

Explorers of the Late Renaissance and the Enlightenment: From Sir Francis Drake to Mungo Park

In earlier centuries, traders and missionaries often proved to also be intrepid explorers, and even during this 250-year period individuals such as fur trader Pierre Gaultier de Varennes et de La Vérendrye and Roman Catholic priest Jacques Marquette were responsible for significant discoveries. The quest for booty, trade, and territory were principal pursuits of many adventurers of the Enlightenment, to be sure, but as the period progressed, the focus of exploration increasingly was on geographical and scientific discovery, with seekers of knowledge for its own sake playing a greater and greater part. Indeed, even though William Dampier was a buccaneer in his early career, he eventually became one of the first Europeans, at least, to travel in order to satisfy his scientific curiosity. Adventurer-scientists who followed Dampier's example included Charles-Marie de La Condamine, in South America, and especially Joseph Banks, who conducted extensive scientific voyages and provided the model for renowned 19th-century naturalists such as Alexander von Humboldt and Charles Darwin.

Despite the great advances in technology and knowledge of the wider world in the 17th and 18th centuries, both overseas and overland exploration remained extremely hazardous. Disease, malnutrition, natural calamities, and confrontations with local inhabitants encountered along the way often proved deadly. It was not until the voyages of James Cook that expeditions provided citrus fruits to eat to prevent scurvy, which had up to then been one of the greatest killers of crew and officers alike on long expeditions. Still, many did not come back from their journeys, notably Vitus Bering, Willem Barents, Henry Hudson, and Cook himself. Their fortitude, perseverance, and willingness to confront the unknown, however, paved the way for the waves of explorers and adventurers who followed them and pushed into the deepest and most remote locales on Earth and eventually left this planet to venture into the vast reaches of space.

GLOSSARY

amity Friendly relations between nations or groups.

ascetic Practicing strict self-denial as a measure of personal and especially spiritual discipline.

boatswain A naval warrant officer in charge of the hull and all related equipment.

buccaneer Any of the freebooters preying on Spanish ships and settlements, especially in 17th-century West Indies.

carte blanche Full discretionary power.

chronometer A timepiece designed to keep time with great accuracy.

collier-bark A ship for transporting coal.

commandant Commanding officer.

conquistador A leader in the Spanish conquest of the Americas and especially of Mexico and Peru in the 16th century.

corsair A privateer of the Barbary Coast.

court-martial To subject members of the armed forces or others within its jurisdiction to trial in front of a court consisting of commissioned officers and in some instances enlisted personnel.

cutter A ship's boat for carrying stores or passengers.

flag rank The rank of any officer in the navy above captain.

frigate A square-rigged war vessel intermediate between a corvette and a ship of the line.

garrison The troops stationed at a military post.

Huguenot Any of the Protestants in France in the 16th and 17th centuries, many of whom suffered severe persecution for their faith.

hustings A raised platform from which candidates for the British Parliament were formerly nominated and from which they addressed their constituency.

hydrographer One specializing in the study of seas, lakes, rivers, and other waters.

magus Sorcerer.

master A ship's officer in charge of navigation.

master's mate A petty naval officer.

merchant marine The commercial ships of a nation, whether privately or publicly owned.

meridian Any of a series of lines drawn at intervals due north and south or in the direction of the poles and numbered according to the degrees of longitude.

midshipman A person in training for a naval commission.

occultation The interruption of the light from a celestial body.

parvenu One that has recently or suddenly risen to an unaccustomed position of wealth or power and has not yet gained the prestige, dignity, or manner associated with it.

philologist One who studies literature and disciplines relevant to literature or language as used in literature.

pinnace A light sailing ship.

plane table An instrument consisting essentially of a drawing board on a tripod with a ruler pointed at the object observed and used for plotting the lines of a survey directly from observation.

polemicist One skilled in the art or practice of disputation or controversy, especially as the advocate of a partisan cause.

privateer Privately owned armed vessel commissioned by a belligerent state to attack enemy ships, usually vessels of commerce; an individual on such a ship.

reconnoitre To make an exploratory or preliminary survey, inspection, or examination of.

restitution A restoration of something to its rightful owner.

sangfroid Self-possession or imperturbability, especially under strain.

seigneur A man of rank or authority.

sextant An instrument for measuring angular distances used especially in navigation to observe altitudes of celestial bodies (as in ascertaining latitude and longitude).

shogun One of a line of military governors ruling Japan, especially between 1603 and 1867.

Spanish Armada The great fleet sent by King Philip II of Spain in 1588 to invade England in conjunction with a Spanish army from Flanders.

survey To make relatively large-scale, accurate measurements of Earth's surfaces.

vicissitude A favourable or unfavourable event or situation that occurs by chance.

BIBLIOGRAPHY

Edward Heawood, *A History of Geographical Discovery in the Seventeenth and Eighteenth Centuries* (1912, reprinted 1965 and 2011), treats exploration during the period in a broad context. Richard Hakluyt, *The Principall Navigations, Voiages, and Discoveries of the English Nation...* (1589, reissued in 2 vol., 1965), also available in an abridged edition, *Voyages and Discoveries*, ed. by Jack Beeching (1972, reissued 1985), contains voluminous information on the early English travels to North America. Later voyages are detailed by E.G.R. Taylor, *Late Tudor and Early Stuart Geography, 1583–1650* (1934, reprinted 1968). Expeditions to the Pacific are chronicled in J.C. Beaglehole, *The Exploration of the Pacific*, 3rd ed. (1966); and Andrew Sharp, *The Discovery of the Pacific Islands* (1960, reprinted 1985). Exploration of the continental interiors is described by John B. Brebner, *The Explorers of North America, 1492–1806* (1964); Margery Perham and J. Simmons (eds.), *African Discovery*, 2nd ed. (1957, reissued 1971); Ernest Scott (ed.), *Australian Discovery*, 2 vol. (1929, reprinted 1966), containing a wide selection of passages from the journals of explorers, with comment; and Günter Schilder, *Australia Unveiled: The Share of Dutch Navigators in the Discovery of Australia* (1976).

Harry Kelsey, *Sir Francis Drake: The Queen's Pirate* (1998), is now the best study of Drake. John Sugden, *Sir Francis Drake* (1990), though superseded by Kelsey, can also be recommended; as can David Beers Quinn, with Burton Van Name Edwards (compiler), *Sir Francis Drake as Seen by His Contemporaries* (1996). Of the many works on Sir Walter Raleigh, William Stebbing, *Sir Walter Ralegh*, 2nd ed. (1899), is a most valuable study; and a solid, newer biography is Raleigh Trevelyan, *Sir Walter Raleigh* (2002). G.M. Asher (ed.), *Henry Hudson the Navigator* (1860, reprinted 1963 and 2007), provides the surviving journals of Hudson's four voyages, supplementary materials, and an important critical introduction. Donald S. Johnson, *Charting the Sea of Darkness: The Four Voyages of Henry Hudson* (1993), is a good biography; and Douglas Hunter, *Half Moon: Henry Hudson and the Voyage That Redrew the Map of the World* (2009), is a more recent account.

Among the many studies of William Penn and his times are Catherine Owens Peare, *William Penn: A Biography* (1956, reissued 1966); and Harry Emerson Wildes, *William Penn* (1974). John Bakeless, *Daniel Boone* (1939, reprinted 1965 and 2008); and John James Van Noppen and Ina Woestemeyer Van Noppen, *Daniel Boone, Backwoodsman* (1966), are standard biographies.

J.C. Beaglehole, *The Life of Captain James Cook* (1974), is a detailed biography; and Alan Villiers, *Captain Cook, the Seamen's Seaman: A Study of the Great Discoverer* (1967, reprinted 2001), is a shorter life study. Historical background of the discoveries and an assessment of their importance are presented in Daniel Conner and Lorraine Miller, *Master Mariner, Capt. James Cook and the Peoples of the Pacific* (1978); and Lynne Withey, *Voyages of Discovery: Captain Cook and the Exploration of the Pacific* (1987).

Works on other Pacific explorers include Andrew Sharp, *The Voyages of Abel Janszoon Tasman* (1968); Ab Hoving and Cor Emke, *The Ships of Abel Tasman* (2000; originally published in Dutch, 2000); John Dunmore (trans. and ed.), *Pacific Explorer: The Life of Jean-François de La Pérouse, 1741–1788* (1985); Douglas Oliver, *Bougainville: A Personal History* (1973); John Dunmore, *Storms and Dreams* (2005), also on Bougainville; Raymond H. Fisher, *Bering's Voyages: Whither and Why* (1977); and Gerhard Friedrich

Müller, *Bering's Voyages: The Reports from Russia*, trans. by Carol Urness (1986; originally published in German, 1758).

Biographies of Champlain include Morris Bishop, *Champlain: The Life of Fortitude* (1948, reprinted 1979); and Samuel Eliot Morison, *Samuel de Champlain, Father of New France* (1972). Louise P. Kellogg (ed.), *Early Narratives of the North-West, 1634–1699* (1917, reprinted 2002), contains translations of original narratives of La Salle's companions; and Francis Parkman, *The Discovery of the Great West*, 5th ed. (1871, reissued in numerous editions), embodies material from La Salle's own letters and other contemporary documents. Francis Borgia Steck, *The Jolliet-Marquette Expedition, 1673* (1928, reprinted 1974), is a standard account of their journeys.

Anton Gill, *The Devil's Mariner: A Life of William Dampier, Pirate and Explorer, 1651–1715* (1997); and Diana Preston and Michael Preston, *A Pirate of Exquisite Mind: Explorer, Naturalist, and Buccaneer: The Life of William Dampier* (2004), discuss this pioneer of scientific travel; while Patrick O'Brian, *Joseph Banks: A Life* (1993), focuses on the early naturalist.Encyclopædia Britannica, Inc.

INDEX

A

Adams, William, 31–33
Africa, 7, 9, 14, 34, 102–103, 119, 120–121
Amazon River, 90
Arabia, 103–104
Arctic region, 22–24, 35–36, 39, 86–87, 92, 97, 110, 112, 113
Australia, 46–47, 54, 55–57, 83, 84, 92, 96, 107–108, 110, 115, 118–119, 122

B

backstaff, 24
Baffin, William, 52
Banks, Sir Joseph, 110–111
Barents, Willem, 22–23, 35, 39
Bass, George, 118–119
Bering, Vitus, 59, 86–87
Bering Strait, 59, 86–87, 92
Boone, Daniel, 104–107
Bougainville, Louis-Antoine de, 99–102
Britain, explorers from, 3–21, 23–39, 45–52, 71–80, 83–85, 91–99, 102–103, 107–122
Bruce, James, 102–103
Button, Sir Thomas, 45–46
Byron, John, 91–92

C

California, 17, 29, 109, 115, 117
Canada
  exploration in, 5, 9, 10, 12, 23, 40, 41–44, 45, 52, 54–55, 60, 61, 62, 64, 66–67, 85, 88–89, 91, 92, 94–95, 111, 113, 115, 117, 118
  explorers from, 88–89
Cavendish, Thomas, 29–30
Champlain, Samuel de, 40–44, 54
Chancellor, Richard, 3–4
circumnavigation of the world, 15–19, 29
Cook, James, 92–99, 109, 111, 115

D

Dampier, William, 83–84
Davis, John, 23–24, 35, 39
Dee, John, 4–6
Denmark, explorers from, 59, 86–87
Dezhnyov, Semyon Ivanov, 59
Diemen, Anthony van, 53–54, 57
Drake, Sir Francis, 7, 9, 10, 12–21, 29, 30
DuLhut, Daniel Greysolon, sieur, 60, 62–63

Index

E

Elizabeth I, 5, 6, 7, 8, 11, 14, 15, 16, 17, 19, 20, 23, 24–25, 27

F

Flinders, Matthew, 122,
Florida, 1–3, 20, 104
Forster, Georg, 114–115
France, explorers from, 40–44, 54–55, 59–71, 81–83, 89–90, 99–102, 108–110, 113
Frobisher, Sir Martin, 5, 9–10

G

Germany, explorers from, 103–104, 114–115
Gilbert, Sir Humphrey, 10–12
Good Hope, Cape of, 19, 29, 46, 84, 115
Greenland, 23–24, 52

H

Hartog, Dirck, 46–47
Hawaii, 99, 109, 117
Hawkins, Sir John, 7–9, 14, 30
Hawkins, Sir Richard, 30–31
Hearne, Samuel, 112–114
Hennepin, Louis, 59–60, 68
Hudson, Henry, 34–39, 45
Hudson's Bay Company, 64, 65, 85, 88, 89, 113, 118

I

Illinois, 60, 62, 68, 69, 83
Indonesia, 53, 84, 96, 101, 120

J

Jamestown Colony, 47–49
Japan, 31, 32–33, 56, 57, 110
Jolliet, Louis, 61, 62, 81–82

K

Kelsey, Henry, 85
Kentucky, 104–105, 106

L

La Condamine, Charles-Marie de, 89–90
La Pérouse, Jean-François de Galaup, comte de, 108–110, 113
La Salle, René-Robert Cavalier, sieur de, 59–60, 65–71, 82
La Vérendrye, Pierre Gaultier de Varennes et de, 88–89
Louisiana, 65, 69, 71, 83, 106
Low Countries, explorers from, 22–23, 35, 46–47, 53–54, 55–58, 59–60

M

Mackenzie, Sir Alexander, 117–118
Magellan, Strait of, 15, 17, 19, 24, 29, 30, 31, 101

Marquette, Jacques, 60–62, 81–82
Menéndez de Avilés, Pedro, 1–3
Michigan, 61, 83
Minnesota, 60, 62, 63
Mississippi River, 60, 61, 62, 63, 64, 65, 68–69, 70, 81–82, 83

N

New England, 50, 51
New Zealand, 54, 55, 57, 92, 96, 97
Nicolet, Jean, 54–55
Niebuhr, Carsten, 103–104
Niger River, 119, 120–1221
Nile River, 102, 103
Northeast Passage, 22, 35
Northwest Passage, 5, 9, 11, 17, 23–24, 35, 37–38, 45, 52, 55, 64, 97, 109

P

Páez, Pedro, 34
Park, Mungo, 119–121
Penn, William, 71–80
Pennsylvania, 71, 76–80
Philip II, 1, 14, 15, 16, 20
Phillip, Arthur, 107–108
Portugal, 11, 21, 53

R

Radisson, Pierre-Esprit, 64–65
Raleigh, Sir Walter, 11, 24–29
Roanoke Island, 27
Russia
  exploration in, 3–4, 86–87, 110
  explorers from, 59

S

slavery, 7, 14
Smith, John, 37, 47–51
Spain, explorers from, 1–3, 34
Spanish Armada campaign, 7, 8–9, 10, 20–21, 24, 30, 31

T

Taiwan, 53, 57
Tasman, Abel Janszoon, 55–58
Tennessee, 104–105
Texas, 70, 71
Tonty, Henri de, 68, 69, 71, 82–83

V

Vancouver, George, 115–117
Venezuela, 27, 28
Virginia, 37, 104, 106

W

West Indies, 1, 7, 9, 10, 14–15, 21, 30, 41, 45, 73, 92, 115
Wisconsin, 54, 55, 61–62, 64, 81

HUNTER HIGH MEDIA CENTER